Navigating the Mortgage Minefield

A partnership between American Library Association
and FINRA Investor Education Foundation

American
Library
Association

Investor Education
FOUNDATION

FINRA is proud to support the American Library Association

Navigating the Mortgage Minefield

Your Complete Guide to Avoiding
Costly Problems and Finding
the Right Loan in Today's Market

RICHARD GIANNAMORE

with

BARBARA BORDOW OSACH

American Management Association
New York • Atlanta • Brussels • Chicago • Mexico City • San Francisco
Shanghai • Tokyo • Toronto • Washington, D.C.

Special discounts on bulk quantities of AMACOM books are available to corporations, professional associations, and other organizations. For details, contact Special Sales Department, AMACOM, a division of American Management Association, 1601 Broadway, New York, NY 10019.
Tel: 212-903-8316. Fax: 212-903-8083.
E-mail: specialsls@amanet.org
Website: www.amacombooks.org/go/specialsales
To view all AMACOM titles go to: www.amacombooks.org

This publication is designed to provide accurate and authoritative information in regard to the subject matter covered. It is sold with the understanding that the publisher is not engaged in rendering legal, accounting, or other professional service. If legal advice or other expert assistance is required, the services of a competent professional person should be sought.

Library of Congress Cataloging-in-Publication Data

Giannamore, Richard, 1941-
   Navigating the mortgage minefield : your complete guide to avoiding costly problems and finding the right loan in today's market / Richard Giannamore with Barbara Bordow Osach.
      p. cm.
   Includes index.
   ISBN-13: 978-0-8144-1369-2
   ISBN-10: 0-8144-1369-2
   1. Mortgage loans—United States.   2. House buying—United States.   I. Osach, Barbara Bordow, 1951–   II. Title.
HG2040.5.U5G542   2009
332.7'20973—dc22

                                        2008055540

Printing number

10 9 8 7 6 5 4 3 2 1

To the men and women who endeavor with integrity
to fulfill their American Dream

Contents

Acknowledgments

Thank you to the many people who contributed their ideas, comments, stories, and support for this book: Special thanks to Ron Giannamore and Don Polletta at Mortgage Services, Inc., who we can count on for creative ideas and unfailing enthusiasm. Their uncompromising stand to empower people to make the changes in their financial habits that enable them to afford homes, and their commitment to provide outstanding service to everyone with whom they come in contact, are an inspiration. Thanks also to Dorothy Suter at Mortgage Services for her review and support, to Nitsan Hargil for his insights into the implications of recent changes, and to Sheila Szymonowicz for sharing her experiences, and to Rose Thomas for her quick and professional response to questions.

Thank you to Mike Snell, our agent, for suggesting and encouraging the book, and for connecting us with Bob Nirkind, our editor at AMACOM. Thanks to Bob for trusting the way we work, and for his suggestions, which invariably improved the clarity and quality of the writing.

From Richard: Thank you to my wife, Paula, for being Paula; generous and loving. And thank you to Barbara for sharing the vision of the difference people make in their lives when they empower themselves.

From Barbara: Thank you to Richard, for the unwavering commitment he is to people having access to freedom, power, and leadership, and for standing, always. And thank you to Patricia Lopes Hargil, who, when things seem dark, is a beacon of light.

EDUCATED BORROWERS ARE OUR
BEST PROTECTION AGAINST BAD
BUSINESS PRACTICES

S ay "the American Dream" and you are likely to envision owning a home as part of that dream. Yet for millions of families who have faced foreclosure home ownership has become a nightmare. In 2008, a presidential election year, the United States Congress passed historic legislation to stimulate and stabilize financial markets that were reeling after the collapse of the subprime mortgage market. In July it approved bills that created a $300 billion fund to rescue the U.S. housing market, bail out home owners at risk of foreclosure, shore up institutions that hold almost half the country's $12 trillion mortgage debt, and impose stricter regulations on the industry. Only three months later, in October, Congress took control of those institutions, and added over $700 billion in funds to absorb the risk of foreclosures, defaults, and bank failures, hoping to stabilize the markets and restore the flow of credit. The message to borrowers: It's dangerous out there!

I have always believed that when people are informed and empower themselves to be responsible for the decisions they make, they rise to the task of knowing what is best for them, and in most cases, they act on it. I've written *Navigating the Mortgage Minefield* to provide the information and straight talk that allows people to empower themselves in this way.

Whether you are thinking of buying a home or refinancing your current home, or if you are searching for a way to avoid foreclosure, you are wise to approach a mortgage mindful of dangers you can avoid if you are informed, alert, and responsible. When you know where you are going, have a road map to guide you, and are in the driver's seat, you can navigate the mortgage minefield and arrive safely at your financial destination.

If you are obtaining a mortgage for the first time, this book takes the mystery out of the mortgage process and provides tools for you to evaluate whether you are truly "ready, willing, and able" to assume the financial responsibilities of home ownership, of which a mortgage is only one part. If you are a veteran of the mortgage process, then the book will help you to brush up on the fine points of the process and establish the mind-set to clearly define and satisfy your present needs effectively and painlessly.

I believe in the power of the free enterprise system to regulate markets, including the mortgage markets. Consumers dictate standards of quality, marketing practices, and product acceptance when they "vote" with their dollars. This book provides the information you need to make informed decisions about the products you buy and the companies from which you buy them. You will engage in the mortgage process fully aware of and responsible for knowing what your obligations are and may become, and what you must do to remain in a position to fulfill your mortgage obligation and other financial commitments.

Educated borrowers and healthy competition between mortgage providers will go further to protect borrowers and markets in the long term than government bailouts, incentives, or regulations. When enough people are informed and responsible, only those organizations and products that responsibly serve the needs of the public will survive in our free enterprise system. You don't have to depend on the government to protect or save you. You can take care of yourself! You have the power!

Not long ago, home owners were regularly bombarded with direct mail, telephone solicitations, and media advertising for mortgages that sounded too good to be true. Zero percent introductory interest rates, 100 percent financing, and promises of "no income verification" lured uninformed borrowers into mortgages that were, in the long run, not the bargains they were touted to be.

Borrowers who thought they could skate through to reasonable refinancing when the "honeymoon" was over on these loans now face monthly mortgage payments they cannot afford. Making matters worse, they have few, if any, options for refinancing, or for selling their homes, which are now worth less than they owe on their mortgages. There is no denying it; the situation is a mess, and for the individuals and families who are struggling, it is deeply upsetting. But is the solution really more government regulation and multibillion--dollar bailouts? Who pays? We all do.

There is nothing inherently wrong, unethical, or deceptive about mortgage products, such as those mentioned earlier, that facilitate home ownership or provide borrowers payment flexibility. These products and others, such as hybrids, home equity lines of credit, and flexible option ARMs, address specific and legitimate market needs. The problem arises not from the product but from the sale of the product to, or use of the product by, someone for whom it is inappropriate and for whom it may cause financial harm. Many people face foreclosure because they were not conscious of or responsible for the risk of conditions that could harm them, and because they were wishful about their current and future financial status, rather than objective and realistic. Many others simply are hard hit by the economic downturn and trying to keep their homes and meet their obligations.

In writing *Navigating the Mortgage Minefield*, I set out to walk prospective borrowers through the thought processes they need to apply information about mortgages to their own financial situation in a manner that develops a responsible appreciation for their capacity to afford a home and honor the terms of a mortgage without hardship and sacrifice.

I've arranged the book to deliver the information that you need to know about mortgages and about yourself as you advance through the mortgage process. The first chapter introduces mortgage products and the mortgage market, and outlines eight important things for you to keep in mind as you navigate the mortgage minefield. Chapter 2 distinguishes between the mortgage for which you may qualify and the mortgage you can afford. It describes all the costs of home ownership, and gives you an unemotional and factual look at your current finances and money habits so you can determine the monthly mortgage payment you can afford.

Chapter 3 discusses situations in which you should consider refinancing, and a method to evaluate whether it makes sense to do it or do nothing. It also provides useful tools to avoid confusion when you compare different offers so you can remain focused on your personal needs and goals.

Chapter 4 helps you to understand what contributes to the value of your current or prospective home and assists you in navigating through some potential hazards related to your property, such as easements and zoning restrictions. It describes circumstances and events that can directly or indirectly affect the value of your home, and explains what you can do to maintain the value of your home and your investment in it.

When you know what you can afford for a mortgage payment, have a budget that includes the multitude of nonmortgage expenses associated with home ownership, and are aware of what to look for in a home to protect your investment in it, you have what you need to enter the mortgage market and take control of your financial future.

Chapter 5 guides you in seeing your financial creditworthiness as lenders see it, and provides you with ways to improve your credit score and other ratios that lenders use to determine whether to lend money to you, and if so, at what cost. Chapter 6 explains basic mortgage products, various features and options available and how you can package them together to create the right loan for you. Chapter 7 helps you to define your financial limits and the objectives you want your mortgage to achieve. It alerts you to mortgage advertising that could lead you astray, and gives you the tools you need to compare offerings to your "shopping list" of mortgage features, rather than trying to compare offers to one another.

Chapter 8 puts you powerfully in charge to find a mortgage professional with whom to do business. The specific questions you ask the mortgage provider about their proposed products and the way they do business allow you to have confidence in the information and advice they give you. The chapter also alerts you to more than ten additional mortgage and financial services of which you can take advantage at little or no cost. Chapter 9 prepares you for the mortgage application process, discussing what questions you will be asked, and why. It explains fees, costs, and the myriad of documents you will sign before you submit your application to a lender for approval. Chapter 10 offers you information about the kinds of insurance you may have to obtain in order for a lender to approve your mortgage. In Chapter 11 you'll receive guidance in reviewing the fine print of the mortgage note and mortgage deed before the closing so you know that what you are signing is what you expected.

We wrap up with the things that can change and actions you should take, both with regard to your specific mortgage (Chapter 12) and in the broader markets (Chapter 13). And finally, in Chapter 14, we address what to do to avoid foreclosure if things go wrong. This chapter alerts you to the pitfalls of negotiating a mortgage modification with your lender, arms you with information about options your lender may not want you to know about, and prepares you to fight to save your home if you face financial distress.

The mortgage and housing markets will rebound, and over the next several decades will slump and rebound again, as they have done historically. The financial markets eventually will stabilize and credit will once again become available for home buyers and home owners. You have the power, and now the tools, to make owning and keeping a home a reality. Regardless of changing market conditions, you'll be able to navigate your way responsibly, so that you can enjoy your home, free from financial struggles. It is my privilege to serve as your guide.

TAKE CHARGE OF YOUR
MORTGAGE PROCESS

When you take charge of your mortgage process, you cannot be pressured or misled by salespeople. You will be able to make decisions based on solid information and a thorough understanding of the terminology and the process itself rather than on your emotions.

This chapter provides you with information you need to understand the different types of mortgages available and the mortgage process. This knowledge, combined with the right attitude, gives you the power to take charge. Being in charge puts you in the driver's seat with a clear road map to reach your financial destination. This chapter is the first step to achieving that power. In it you will learn:

☑ How a mortgage balances risk and reward

☑ What the elements of a mortgage are and what payment options are available

☑ What the steps in the mortgage process are

☑ Eight things to keep in mind when searching for a mortgage

Balancing Risk and Reward in a Mortgage

Lending money involves a balance between risk and reward. The lender's risk is that the borrower will not repay. A lender's reward is the interest the borrower pays for the use of the money. Borrowing money for a mortgage also involves a balance between risk and reward. As a borrower, your reward is the home you enjoy. Your risk is that if you are unable to pay you could lose your home. Understanding the risks is the first step in determining the right balance of risk and reward for your situation.

A *mortgage* is a loan to finance real estate. In the most basic sense it is the price of risk and the cost of security. The real estate property "secures" the loan, and the mortgage gives the lender a *lien* against the property. This means that if you don't pay the loan back according to its terms the lender has the right to take the property from you, sell it, and recover the debt you owe from the proceeds of the sale.

Is debt bad? Debt incurred for expenses or purchases of items that do not grow in value (for example, dinner at a restaurant or the purchase of an automobile) diminishes your financial position. Debt incurred to invest in something that increases in value is called *leverage* and is a powerful wealth-building tool.

Let's do the math. If you have $20,000 in cash, you have an asset worth $20,000. If you use that $20,000 as a down payment on a $100,000 house, you will need an $80,000 mortgage. You now have a $100,000 asset (the house) offset by the $80,000 liability (the mortgage), leaving you with net assets of $20,000. So far your net financial position is unchanged, other than the interest you have paid for the use of the $80,000. If, however, real estate values go up, and your house is worth $120,000 two years after you bought it, you are in a better financial position. For simplicity sake, let's say you still owe the full $80,000 on the mortgage (in reality you probably will have paid back a small part of it). Your net assets are now $40,000 ($120,000 minus $80,000). You've doubled your net assets by taking out a mortgage on a property that has appreciated in value. That's leverage.

Another way of looking at it is that if you put $20,000 down on a $100,000 property and it appreciates at 8 percent, you have a very respectable return of $8,000, less the interest you paid for the use of the money, on your $20,000 investment—a 16 percent return!

Any opportunity for wealth building is risky. Historically and in general, real estate appreciates or grows in value over time. But there are no guarantees that the home you buy, at the time you buy it, and for the price you pay, will appreciate in value by the time you are ready to sell it. If property values decline, your net assets will shrink and you could lose your $20,000 and more. Using the numbers in the previous example, if the real estate values in your area decline, and if at the end of the two years your property is only worth $95,000 instead of the $100,000 you paid for it, your net assets are now $15,000 ($95,000 minus $80,000) and, if you sold your home, you will have lost $5,000 on your investment after paying off the $80,000 mortgage. Take into account, however, that you enjoyed the use of your home and avoided paying rent for those two years, so you are still ahead financially.

Is the risk of declining real estate values a reason not to buy a home or take a mortgage? NO! It is the reason you should be very clear about the terms of the mortgage and understand the risk. The terms of your mortgage will be determined by the lender's assessment of risk and reward. As you continue to read this chapter you will learn how the lender makes that assessment, what affects property values and how to assess the likelihood of your property increasing or decreasing in value over time. You will also understand when and by how much your mortgage payments could change. And you will be able to make a responsible decision that meets both your short- and long-term financial goals and is within your emotional tolerance for risk.

Assessing the Lender's Risk

The lender assesses the risk that you will pay the mortgage on time against the value of the property should you default, and determines how much money is required to assume that risk. This section examines three key factors—property value, your credit, and your monthly income—that a lender considers when deciding whether to lend you money, and if so, how much it will cost you. A lender sometimes considers other factors as well in a mortgage transaction, but these three are foremost in determining whether you qualify for a mortgage, and if so, how much you will pay for it.

Property Value. Since your property secures the mortgage, the value of your property compared to the amount of your loan is very important to the lender. The lender wants a cushion between the value of the property and the amount you borrow, so that if property values decline and you fail to pay, the lender still will be able to sell the property and recover the amount you owe. The amount of the loan as a percentage of the value of the property is called the *loan to value (LTV) ratio.*

To get the most favorable lending terms, the amount you borrow should not exceed 80 percent of the value of your home. You may be able to borrow a higher percentage, but you will be required to pay more in interest and *private mortgage insurance (PMI)*. PMI is additional insurance to protect the lender if you default. Depending on the economy and lending climate, 100 percent financing could be available, and in some cases you could qualify for a loan that is greater than the value of your home.

If you are purchasing a home, the lender asks the amount of your down payment and from what source those funds will come. The lender's interest in the source of your down payment is based on the impact it will have on your ability to pay the mortgage. If you borrow the down payment from relatives or borrow against other assets, the lender takes into account that repayment obligation when assessing your income. If you have saved money for a down payment, the lender knows that the assets you currently have will be reduced by the amount you use for the down payment.

The value of the property is the security on your loan. You can get an estimate of your home's value from your real estate agent, or from free online services such as www.zillow.com, but the value of your property for purposes of the loan is determined by an appraisal. An *appraisal* is an assessment by a professional (appraiser) that compares the recent sale prices and real estate assessments of houses of similar age, size, and location to your property to estimate the price at which you could sell your home (or more to the point, the amount for which the lender could sell your home if you default on your loan). If the appraised value is not within an acceptable range of the purchase price of the house, the lender may ask for additional information regarding other assets that you may have, or may decline to provide funding.

Credit. When you make credit transactions (such as credit card purchases, loans, or store charge cards), in most cases the vendor reports the transaction to credit bureaus that make the information available to lenders in a credit report. Your credit report says a lot about you as an individual. It tells the lender if you are trustworthy based on a number of facts. The credit report includes a calculated credit score designed to allow the lender to make a quick judgment about your ability to manage and meet your credit obligations. It also tells the lender how much you owe, how much money others are willing to lend you (your credit limits), how much of your credit limit is still available to you, and whether you make your payments on time.

Your credit score is one of the single biggest factors that determine how costly your mortgage will be. Scores range from 350 to 850. Scores above 759 are excellent, and give you access to the lowest interest rates. Scores below 580 make it very difficult to obtain a mortgage you can afford, and if someone is willing to give you the money, you will have to pay a premium for it. If your score is in the range of 640 to 720, rates will fluctuate with the mood of the financial markets. During a lending boom, scores in this range qualified you for rates near those available for borrowers with excellent credit scores. As money markets tightened, lenders began using credit scores to calculate interest rate premiums; the lower the credit score, the higher the rate. Poor credit or no credit history will hurt you. If your credit score is below 580, you will pay a higher interest rate and/or closing costs (points).

Several things can bring your credit score down. Late payments on a mortgage or automobile loan are particularly damaging, and lenders weigh these "lates" heavily against you. "Maxing out" your credit cards by borrowing the full amount of your credit limit also reduces your credit score. By law you are entitled to a free copy of your credit report once a year. If you don't know what your credit score is or what your credit history tells prospective lenders, request a copy and read it. You can receive a free copy and analysis of your credit report at my company's website, www.tomortgageservices.com. If you believe it is inaccurate, take action to have it corrected. Chapter 5 explains the credit report in detail, and ways to improve your credit score.

Income. The third factor lenders consider when deciding to lend you money is your monthly income. Lenders compute two ratios based on your income: Housing ratio and debt to income ratio. The *housing ratio* is the percentage of your monthly income that is required (or will be required) to pay the mortgage and interest and the expenses needed to protect the value of the property and the lender's right to sell it should you default: real estate taxes, home owner's insurance, condominium fees and, if required, PMI. PMI is required when your loan to value ratio is greater than 80 percent, and it insures the lender if you default. The *debt to income ratio* is the percentage of your income needed to pay your housing expense and your other credit obligations.

A housing ratio of 28 percent and debt to income ratio of 36 percent or less will get you the best rate on your mortgage. Other favorable factors, such as a large reserve of savings or investments, can offset higher than desired ratios when a lender is evaluating your loan application. These assets tell the lender that you are able to manage your money, and that you have access to extra funds if you need them to meet your monthly obligations.

The bigger the risk you are to the lender, the more you pay for a mortgage. The cost of a mortgage is reflected in the rate of interest and in the "points" you will pay. The interest rate is the amount you will pay for the use of the money over the life or "term" of the loan, in addition to the loan amount. *Points* are a one-time fee, a percentage of the amount you borrow, that is paid at the time the money is borrowed. You can reduce the interest rate by increasing the points. If you are a relatively high risk, the lender could also impose PMI as a condition of the loan. All these additional costs make the risk financially acceptable to the lender.

Assessing Your Risks

Just as the lender assesses the risk factors related to your mortgage, you should assess the risk of changes in your ability to make the payments, and changes in the value of your home. Property value, income, and credit load are all important factors.

No one likes to think that they suddenly could be out of a job, but people get laid off or fired all the time. No one likes to think that they could be unemployed for many months, but it happens, and people have to tap into savings or retirement accounts to carry them through the rough times.

No one likes to think that the value of their property will decline, but many of the factors that determine property values are not within the control of home owners. For example, the local economy can change drastically, creating a glut of houses for sale. The quality of schools, nearby development, availability of local services, and real estate taxes all have an impact on property values as well.

In addition to the lender's risk criteria, also consider your tolerance for risk. Your home should be a source of enjoyment, not a cause for constant stress and concern. You may be very uncomfortable with uncertainty or change, in which case a monthly payment that does not change may be the best choice for you. On the other hand, you may be perfectly comfortable with a "calculated" risk, and are willing to bet that the future will be favorable, in order to take advantage of mortgages that start low but may rise.

Navigating the Mortgage Minefield: Think Longer Term

Some of the dangers you face in the process of obtaining a mortgage are external, such as the salesmanship of mortgage originators or the advice of well-intentioned but ill-informed friends and family. But one of the biggest dangers is your own thinking, particularly when it is strongly influenced by your emotional attachment to what you want now. When it comes to buying a home they absolutely love, people tend to overemphasize their immediate wants and don't consider or underestimate the likelihood of events that could interfere with their ability to meet their mortgage obligations. When you let your emotions dictate your decisions, you will justify the decision you want to make, rather than realistically think through the longer-term risks and consequences. To safely navigate the mortgage minefield, think longer-term.

Here are some mortgage-related examples of dangerous short-term thinking:

☑ I know this monthly payment will leave me a little tight, but I will be getting a raise next year, and I can "tighten my belt" until then.

☑ The introductory interest rate is manageable, and I can always refinance before the rate goes up.

☑ The bank is willing to lend me that much, so I must be able to afford it.

Millions of people have been blindsided by circumstances that proved their hopeful assumptions about the future false. Your company issues a wage freeze or, worse yet, you lose your job. (Don't think it could happen to you? Are you willing to bet your home on it?) When it comes time to refinance at the end of your introductory period, the value of your property is not sufficient to refinance at a lower rate, or lenders have tightened their underwriting guidelines and you are not able to qualify. The company stock that makes up the bulk of your reserves "tanks," drastically shrinking your nest egg. Unexpected expenses, such as medical bills or automobile repairs, increase your debt and the related minimum monthly payments.

Don't be tempted to indulge in short-term thinking with long-term rosy hopefulness. The most important thing is to be honest with yourself, and to be responsible for your decisions.

The Elements of a Mortgage

All mortgages have a few things in common. You borrow an amount called the principal for a length of time called the term, and you pay the lender for the use of the money at a specified interest rate. Mortgages either have a fixed rate of interest, or an adjustable rate. In addition, a mortgage is a lien against your property that gives the lender the right to foreclose and sell your house if you fail to pay the mortgage.

Common Mortgage Definitions

All mortgages begin with the principal. The loan *principal* is the amount of money you borrow. If you are buying a house for $150,000 and you have a down payment of $25,000, and you want a mortgage for the balance, your principal amount would be $125,000.

The *term* of the loan is the length of time over which you will repay it. Most fixed-rate mortgages are fifteen or thirty years. Most adjustable-rate mortgages also have a term of thirty years. The term often is expressed in months; a thirty-year mortgage has a 360-month term.

The *interest rate* is the percentage of the principal amount that you will repay to the lender, in addition to the principal that you borrow. The interest rate percentage can either remain the same for the entire time you borrow the money (*fixed rate*) or it may change from time to time at agreed-upon intervals (*variable* or *adjustable rate*).

Your *monthly payment* is the amount of principal and interest you will be required to pay each month over the term of your loan. For a fixed-rate mortgage, the monthly payment remains the same for the entire loan term. With an adjustable-rate mortgage, the monthly principal and interest may change. In addition to the principal and interest, you may be required to pay PMI to the lender. The lender also requires that you assume other expenses such as property taxes, condominium fees if applicable, and hazard insurance. The lender may collect money for these items from you monthly and hold it in a special *escrow account* from which the lender will pay the bills, or you may be allowed to pay them directly.

The dollar amount of interest that you will repay on your loan is not a straight calculation. The longer the term for which you borrow the money, the more interest you will pay. For example, if you borrow $100,000 for thirty years at 6.5 percent interest, you will actually pay back $227,520, of which $127,520 is the interest amount. If you borrow the same $100,000 at 6.5 percent for fifteen years, you will pay only $56,780 in interest.

At the end of the loan term, the loan principal and interest are fully paid off. This is referred to as *full amortization*. However, unlike a car loan, you cannot simply take your total principal and interest amount and divide it equally by the number of monthly payments to calculate the balance remaining on the loan. With a four-year car loan, you will have repaid half the principal at the end of two years. With a mortgage, the repayment schedule is structured to pay most of the interest amount before paying the principal. For most of the loan term, a large percentage of the monthly payment will be applied to the interest amount, and only a small portion will reduce the loan amount. Toward the end of the loan, most of the monthly payment will be applied to the principal balance. This is important for you to know if you are likely to sell your home or refinance your home before the term is up. On a thirty-year mortgage, you will have repaid about 27.5 percent of the principal after fifteen years. If you sell or refinance, you still owe the remaining principal balance to the lender. Most home owners turn over a mortgage either because of a sale or a refinance every seven to ten years.

Adjustable-Rate Mortgage Definitions

If you consider an *adjustable-rate mortgage (ARM)*, you should understand the general terms related to ARMs and be fully aware of the specifics of your adjustable-rate mortgage.

ARMs start with an *initial interest rate*. Typically the initial interest rate is lower than the prevailing fixed rates that are offered at the same time. For example, if the prevailing rate for fixed-rate loans is 6.5 percent, on the same day an ARM introductory rate for the same term could be 5.25 percent. When you buy a fixed-rate mortgage you pay extra for protection against rising interest rates, and the lender assumes all the risk. The lender also reaps all the benefit if interest rates fall. With an ARM, the risk is shared, and both lender and borrower are affected by rises and declines in prevailing interest rates.

The initial interest rate remains in effect for an *initial fixed period*. Depending on the ARM, the initial fixed period could be as long as ten years or as short as one month. At the end of the initial fixed period, your interest rate can be adjusted upward or downward. The maximum size of the adjustment is defined in the mortgage agreement as the *initial rate cap*.

The adjusted interest rate is based on one of several economic indices. The *index* to which the rate is tied varies with lending institution, and generally is not negotiable. You can learn more about the performance of common indices at www.mortgage-x.com/general/mortgage_indexes.asp. Your interest rate includes an additional percentage by which the index is increased, called the *margin*. Margins vary from lender to lender, but usually are consistent over the term of the loan.

The ARM also defines how often the adjustments can be made. This is called an *adjustment period*. There may be an *initial adjustment period* at the end of the initial fixed period, followed by subsequent adjustment periods. For example, in a 5/1 ARM the initial adjustment period is five years, and typically the subsequent adjustment period is every year after that.

There are several "caps," or maximums, defined in the ARM. The *periodic rate cap* determines how much the interest rate can increase in any one adjustment. This protects you (presumably) from being suddenly faced with extreme increases in your monthly payments. Be warned, however, that if your current payments are merely comfortable or a little tight, any increase can become a financial burden.

The *life-time rate cap* defines the maximum increase in interest rate you will ever pay. No matter how high the index goes, your interest rate will never exceed your initial interest rate plus the life-time rate cap. For example, if your initial interest rate is 5 percent and your life-time cap rate is 7 percent, then your maximum interest rate is 12 percent. This is your worst-case scenario, and you should know what your monthly mortgage payment could be under the worst conditions. If you cannot afford that monthly payment and go ahead with the mortgage betting (or hoping) that the cap will never be reached, understand that you are betting that your income will rise or that you will be able to refinance to a lower rate at the time your ARM is adjusted to the life-time rate cap percentage. If you lose the bet, you could lose your home.

The *initial rate cap* defines the maximum jump from the initial rate to the first adjusted rate. It may not be the same as the *periodic rate cap* that applies to subsequent adjustment periods. In fact, the initial rate cap could equal the life-time cap. This means that at the end of the initial period your interest rate could jump in one step from a low introductory rate to the worst-case scenario, and remain there until the next adjustment period. It is important that you know the terms of your ARM and what the effect on your monthly payment could be after each adjustment. Avoid surprises.

The *payment cap* defines the maximum amount of your monthly payment. You might think this could only work in your favor, but you would be mistaken. If the life-time cap results in a payment that exceeds the payment cap, your monthly payment will not lower your principal balance. In fact, your payment cap could result in a monthly payment that is too low to cover the interest due for the month. If that is the case, the amount you owe increases, rather than decreases, with every payment. You may or may not be able to make additional payments without penalty to avoid this situation.

Finally, some loans come with a prepayment penalty. This means that if you sell your home or refinance your home before the loan term expires, the lender can penalize you with large fees. If you accept (or have no choice but to accept) a loan with a prepayment penalty, you will have to factor the cost of the penalty into the price of a new mortgage.

Having said all this, you may now be terrified to consider ARMs. Don't be. Can they be dangerous? Without a doubt. They can also be a very shrewd financial tool when used in the right circumstances: by responsible borrowers who know exactly what they are getting into. Many of the ARMs with long initial periods (three, five, seven, or ten years), are known as *hybrids*, and they combine the stability of a fixed-rate with the lower introductory rates of an ARM. Hybrids are referred to using expressions such as "3/1" or "5/1," where the first number indicates the number of years for which the interest rate is fixed, and the second number indicates the frequency, in years, of adjustments following the initial fixed period. A hybrid is an excellent choice for borrowers who know they are going to sell or refinance before the expiration of the initial period.

Payment Options

Both fixed-rate and adjustable-rate mortgages can offer a variety of payment options for all or part of the term. An *interest-only payment* is a payment that covers the interest due for the payment period, but includes no principal. *Minimum payments* are defined by the mortgage agreement, and may be less than interest-only payments. Interest-only and minimum payments, while saving you money in the short term, can be very costly in the long run, resulting in an increase in the amount you repay on the loan rather than a decrease. This is known as *negative amortization*. Remember that the longer the term for which you borrow money, the more you will repay in interest. If you are not paying off principal with each payment, you are paying interest on some part of the principal for a longer time. And if you are making a minimum payment that does not even cover the interest, then you actually are adding the unpaid interest to the balance of the loan, and you will be paying additional interest on the unpaid interest. It is not difficult to see how you can get yourself into real financial trouble if you do not use these flexible payment options responsibly.

The Mortgage Process

To take charge of your mortgage experience you must understand the basic process you will go through to obtain a loan. The mortgage industry is big business. There are many national lenders with access to billions of dollars in funds. There are also many individual players; independent salespeople who generate business and originate loans. Every party involved in the process of obtaining a residential mortgage is in business, and to stay in business they have to make a profit.

Why is this important for you to know? Unless you are clear about what the people with whom you are dealing are trying to accomplish, you can easily misplace your trust and abdicate your responsibility to make decisions that are in your best interest. Does that mean you shouldn't trust people? No. The best in the industry—the ones who can weather good financial times and difficult financial times—know that their long-term success depends on doing what is best for their customers. But it is also up to you to know what is best for you. Leave that to someone else and you could have a financial disaster on your hands, or you could end up paying more than you need to for your financing.

If you are buying a home, you have to know the price range of the homes you can afford and for which you will be able to obtain financing. Chapter 2 provides tools that will assist you in deciding how much you can afford. You can take the guesswork out of the amount of financing you can obtain by getting preapproved by a lender. Preapproval is a process in which a lender determines how much you can borrow before you apply for a loan on a specific property. When a lender preapproves you for a mortgage, you have a high degree of certainty that any home you want to buy that fits the basic parameters of the preapproval will be funded, assuming there are no significant changes to your income or credit.

If you are purchasing a home, you may work with a real estate agent or broker. Both are real estate professionals. An agent works for a broker, and brokers are licensed to manage their own real estate businesses. The agent or broker shows you houses for sale, based on the price range and other information you provide. Agents and brokers sell houses to people who can pay for them (usually through a mortgage), for sellers who pay them a commission. Your preapproval tells the real estate professionals that you are a serious prospect, and that if they can find a home in your price range that you like, financing will not be an obstacle to closing the deal. A preapproved buyer is also attractive to a seller, who does not want to see a deal fall through because the buyer cannot get financing, especially if other offers have been turned away.

The agent or broker you work with may represent you and your interests, but the commission is usually paid by the seller, and is included in the price of the home. Agents and brokers do not earn a commission if you don't buy, so they are motivated to show you homes you can afford. On the other hand, the higher the price of the home, the more commission the real estate agent or broker earns. Consequently, you should not be surprised if they steer you to homes priced at the high end of your range, or even a little higher.

Once you find the home you want and your offer is accepted by the seller, you need a loan originator, mortgage broker, or lender through which to obtain financing. *Loan originators* (also known as *mortgage originators*) are the mortgage professionals who take your application, obtain and analyze your credit report, and propose a particular type of mortgage for you, at a specific price. *Mortgage brokers* are people who bring borrowers and lenders together, and they earn a fee for doing so. *Lenders* are the organizations that determine the terms of your loan and provide the funds in exchange for a security interest in your property.

Your best source is a referral from someone you trust who has had a firsthand positive experience with a mortgage professional. Your real estate agent or broker may be able to recommend someone with whom they have worked before, but shop around.

Whether seeking preapproval, applying for a new home loan, or refinancing an existing one, the mortgage process begins by completing an application form, called a 1003 (pronounced ten-oh-three). The form asks for information about your current housing expenses, your income, and your assets such as savings and retirement accounts. It also asks for identity information such as social security number and date of birth so a detailed credit report can be obtained. If you have already made an offer on a property, or if you are refinancing your home, information about the value and condition of the property for which the mortgage is being obtained also will be required.

Loan originators use your application to obtain your credit report, and analyze your income, housing expense, and credit to get a sense for how your application will be viewed by a lender. The originator should also ask you questions about your plans for staying in the house, about your job, and your short- and long-term financial objectives, particularly if you are refinancing. In addition, they arrange to have the property appraised. Loan originators either work directly for a lender, or for a mortgage broker. Many are paid a commission based on loan profit, or on a "per loan" basis.

An *appraisal* of the property being mortgaged is conducted by a trained and certified professional *appraiser*. The appraiser determines the value of the property based on recent sales of similar properties in similar neighborhoods under similar market conditions. He or she issues an appraisal report that details the comparisons and the method used to determine the value of your property. You pay the appraiser a fee, which can vary depending on the value of the property.

The appraised value should be very close to your purchase price, unless unusual circumstances cause the property to be discounted or sold at a premium. For example, the purchase price could be lower than the appraised value of the home if the seller is being forced to sell due to a job relocation or divorce. On the other hand, if the home is very desirable in a market where there are few desirable homes available for sale, the seller may demand and will likely receive a premium over the house's appraised value. Question and understand fully significant discrepancies between the appraised value and the purchase price of the home you are buying.

Based on your financial needs and goals, the information obtained from your mortgage application, credit report, and appraisal, the originator reviews your options, and explains the risks and benefits of different mortgage products for which you qualify in terms of your stated goals. Good loan originators make certain you understand the process and the criteria by which your creditworthiness is being evaluated, and how that impacts the price of your loan. They take the time to ask questions about your financial goals, and to answer any questions you have about the process or about the loans they are recommending. They may also recommend ways for you to improve your numbers so you can qualify for a less expensive loan.

Once a loan originator knows your financial standing and goals, a broker will search the money market for the most attractive terms available to you. Brokers typically have access to hundreds of mortgage wholesalers—lenders who do not deal directly with borrowers—and so have a wide variety of packages they may be able to offer to you. Brokers make their money on fees that are included in the cost of the mortgage. These fees cover the cost of the loan origination, administration, and processing.

Some loan originators do not work through brokers; they are employed directly by lenders such as banks. In that case, the loan originator will find a loan for you from among the mortgages that lender offers. Guidelines vary among lenders, and if any of your ratios are close to the limits or below optimal, you should shop around if you are dealing directly with a lender. The mortgage broker does that shopping for you on the wholesale market.

If you decide to move forward, the originator prepares a package of application documents for you to review and sign, and submits the application package to the lender on your behalf. You may be required to pay an application fee at this time. If the mortgage originator works for a bank or other retail lending institution, the application package goes to another department for underwriting. If the loan originator is affiliated with or works for a mortgage broker, he or she submits the loan package to a wholesale lender for underwriting.

An *underwriter* is someone you are not likely to meet, but who makes the final determination about whether to offer you a loan, and if so, at what cost. Industry guidelines determine whether the loan is salable on the secondary market, and the lender for whom the underwriter works has guidelines and conditions that must be met. The underwriter makes the decision based on your loan application, your credit report, the appraisal, and other documents he or she may request of you. Once the underwriter is satisfied that you are a good credit risk, your loan is cleared to close and the closing is scheduled. You should then have an option to "lock" the rate at which the mortgage was approved. This protects you against increasing interest rates in the market between the time of your approval and your closing.

The *closing* is the event at which all final documents for the mortgage and, in the case of a purchase, transfer of property ownership are signed and money changes hands between mortgage holders, buyers, and sellers. In the case of a refinance, the closing marks the beginning of a three-day waiting period, known as a *rescission period*, before funds are released and the new mortgage holder is officially put on record with a lien against the property.

Attorneys may represent the seller, the buyer, and the lender in a mortgage transaction and closing. While not required in some states, representation by an attorney is not unusual. An attorney or other "settlement agent" prepares the closing documents. Among those documents is the mortgage note, which is the contract between the borrower and the lender. All terms and conditions are specified in the mortgage note, including the conditions under which the lender can foreclose.

Eight Things to Keep in Mind When Searching for a Mortgage

There is no need for you to become an expert in order to avoid potential minefields in the mortgage process, but you are responsible for determining what is best for you. The greatest danger you face is abdicating that responsibility to someone else. These eight tips will guide you and empower you to make an informed decision when obtaining your mortgage.

1. The Cost of Owning a Home Is More than the Cost of the Mortgage, Taxes, and Insurance

Owning a home is expensive, and it costs you time or money or both to keep it in good condition. When you own your own home, you are your own landlord and building superintendent. Expenses the landlord may have paid, such as water, sewer connections, and taxes, maintenance, and repairs on the structure and appliances are now your responsibility. If the pipes spring a leak, you either fix it yourself or pay someone to do it. When you move into your first home, you should also be prepared for some major expenses or to negotiate with the seller for things like a refrigerator, washer, and dryer.

2. Just Because You Qualify for a Loan Doesn't Mean You Can Afford It

Underwriting guidelines tighten and relax as national economic and political climates change. Lenders are interested in the specific measures of risk described earlier, but they do not account for all of your financial obligations or goals. A lender will not know or factor in the fact that you are saving money to fund your children's college or your own retirement. Lenders look at your savings and investments to determine how long you could continue paying the mortgage if you lose your job or are unable to work. Don't be lured into a bigger monthly commitment than you can comfortably handle. Your home should be a source of enjoyment, not constant stress.

3. Lenders Are in the Mortgage Business to Make a Profit

There is nothing wrong with making a profit; the American economy depends on it. It is up to you to know how the parties you are dealing with are compensated, and whether they are gouging you or making a fair profit on the transaction. You must learn to understand the numbers and evaluate the value of the transaction against the cost. You must also learn what to look for in a mortgage company to give you assurances that profit is fair and the transaction is beneficial to you. The information you need to understand and assess the transaction terms is contained in Chapters 6 and 7.

4. Things Change, and Sometimes You Have Control and Sometimes You Don't

Life can throw us curve balls, and sometimes we have very little control over the circumstances with which we have to deal. You can perform very well at work, but your company may be forced to lay you off based on factors other than performance. Money markets tighten and you may be unable to refinance. The important thing to remember as you shop for a mortgage is that almost nothing stays the same for thirty years (the typical term of a mortgage). You should not assume that your income will remain the same, that your credit will remain the same, or that your property value will remain the same. You will have to make assumptions about each of those factors. It is important that you know they are assumptions, not certainties, and that they carry a certain degree of risk. The question to keep asking is "What if my assumption is not accurate? What is the risk? Is it worth it?" Think long-term. A mortgage is a long-term financial commitment, and real estate is a long-term financial investment. Your immediate wants and desires, if they overshadow the prudence of long-term thinking, can cost you a lot of money. Understand that the information you provide during the loan application process is used to make judgments about the timing and likelihood of your mortgage lasting its full term. You are responsible for the accuracy of that information and for understanding what your answers mean in terms of the right options and loan features for you.

5. The Best Mortgage Is Not Necessarily the One with the Lowest Interest Rate and Points

Mortgage pricing is a complex combination of interest rates, points, and closing costs that can be presented in a deceptively simplistic manner to make them seem quite attractive. Before the recent mortgage industry downturn, lenders heavily advertised interest rates as low as 1 percent. Those rates represented interest-only or minimum payments for a short period. If you are attracted to that kind of loan without fully understanding the future ramifications of your choice, you could lose your home. If a loan sounds too good to be true, it probably is; look for the hidden costs or catches. As you read this book, you will learn more about mortgage pricing and how to compare loans to make the right decision for yourself.

6. Lenders Get Their Money from the Same Sources

The mortgage business is fundamentally a huge market for buying and selling money. Long gone are the days when your local bank provided loans on the basis of the assets it held from depositors.

These days the money available for mortgages is determined primarily on the securities-backed bond market. This means that your local bank and every other mortgage lender obtains the funds they lend from the same money markets. Lenders compete with one another for the funds.

Funds become available to lenders when they sell the mortgages on the secondary market. The largest purchasers of loans on the secondary market are Fannie Mae (Federal National Mortgage Association) and Freddie Mac (Federal Home Loan Mortgage Corporation), lending institutions that were once independent *government-sponsored enterprises (GSEs)* and are now run by the U.S. Treasury and Federal Financing Housing Agency. Fannie Mae and Freddie Mac bundle the loans they buy and sell them on the financial markets, as mortgage-backed securities, to replenish their availability of funds. They are backed by the U.S. government, and so the mortgage-backed securities they offer on the bond markets were at one time considered to be among the lowest risks in the money markets. Based on the perceived risk of the pool of loans being offered, the interest rates the lenders pay for their money rise or fall.

Fannie Mae and Freddie Mac set standards for loan underwriting, and only if a mortgage "conforms" to those guidelines will they buy the loan from the originating lender, thereby replenishing the lender's availability of funds.

What does this all mean to you? No matter the lender with which you deal, your credit history, income, and property value will qualify you for mortgages in a fairly narrow range of terms. A thirty-year fixed will cost you about the same amount no matter from which reputable party you obtain it. If the costs vary widely, keep shopping; you can almost be certain that someone is trying to get rich on your loan, and you should go elsewhere. Never think that you are stuck doing business with someone just because they have a mortgage for which you qualify. If you can get it from them, you can get it elsewhere, and when you understand more about mortgage pricing and costs, as you will after reading this book, you will be able to compare offers and make a decision with a high degree of confidence.

7. You Are in Charge

Ask advice of experts and listen to the advice of friends and family, if you must. Trust the people with whom you are going to do business. But be responsible for knowing what you are doing, to what you are agreeing, and what commitments you are making for yourself and your family when you sign a mortgage note. Ask questions. If you don't understand the answer, ask again. And again. Ask as many times as necessary until you understand it well enough to explain it to someone else. No matter how embarrassed you might feel asking for explanations more than once, imagine the embarrassment of a foreclosure because you failed to understand the terms of your commitment and are no longer able to meet them. Take the time to understand everything.

8. No Is Not Forever

If you fail to qualify for a mortgage, there are actions you can take to improve your finances so that in the future you can qualify for a loan with terms you can afford. Time is on your side if you take steps to improve your credit and loan ratios. Even in a rising real estate market (which we will see again), it is never too late to buy a home. Never let the fear of never being able to afford a home rush you into a bad financial or investment decision. Another house will always come along. Wait to buy a home you can afford rather than put your family into financial jeopardy by overstretching or overpaying for a mortgage.

Time and again people come into our offices to refinance mortgages they obtained elsewhere, and when we look at the terms and look at their finances, we know they have been paying more for a mortgage than they needed to. Fortunately for many of them, we are able to get them into a new mortgage that better meets their needs. When we ask why they had agreed to certain terms, too often the answer is "I didn't realize I had a choice." Or "I didn't know." We don't want that happening to you. So continue to read this book and get ready to take charge.

BE REALISTIC ABOUT BEING ABLE
TO AFFORD A HOME

Deciding to buy a home is not only a financial decision, but a very personal one. For most people it is primarily a lifestyle decision that has financial ramifications, rather than a financial decision with lifestyle consequences. While it is critical to take the finances into account, the decision to buy a home is more complex than the cost per square foot of living space or the return on financial investment. The noneconomic factors have very real economic consequences. The right decision combines financial facts, emotional considerations, and an honest assessment of your financial habits and lifestyle preferences.

This chapter provides tools to help you determine what you can afford. In it you will learn:

☑ How to set up a realistic budget and stick to it

☑ How a lender sees your finances

☑ How you can take advantage of prequalification and preapproval services

☑ What the added expenses of home ownership compared to renting are

☑ What special programs and incentives are available to first-time home buyers

☑ What other costs and expenses may affect you and your home

Set a Realistic Budget and Stick to It

Before you consider buying a home, look at your current finances with an objective eye. Be honest with yourself about your spending and saving habits, your ability to handle credit responsibly, and your current ability to manage your finances comfortably. Are you contributing to savings regularly? Do you pay your bills on time? Are your credit card balances paid in full each month or is your debt growing?

A budget is one of the most effective tools you have to assess your financial habits and control your finances. If you have not put together a budget, create one before you consider buying a home. If you already have a budget but find it difficult to stick to it, buying a home could be disastrous.

A *budget* is a detailed estimate and accounting of all your monthly income and expenses, by category. The best budgets take everything into account, including expenses that do not occur on a monthly or planned basis. For example, if you go to the dentist twice a year, a good budget takes the annual cost of your two visits (for instance, $90 each visit), and divides it by twelve, for a monthly dental expense budget of $15. If you are responsible and truly stick to your budget, you put that $15 into a savings account each month so that you have the money to pay your bill even before your appointment occurs. Most people do not manage their money this way, but those who do are able to get the most favorable mortgage terms, and can more easily weather unexpected expenses with peace of mind.

To formulate a budget, you need to know how much money you earn, and how much you spend for what items. Table 2-1 provides a list of general categories for budgeting. If your income is irregular because of tips, commissions, bonuses, or overtime, estimate your monthly income by taking your total income for the last two years and dividing by twenty-four. Go back one full year and record and classify all of your spending into one of the categories shown, or create additional categories as needed. If you cannot reconstruct your income or spending habits, you may not be ready for the financial responsibility of home ownership.

Once you know what your income and expenses historically have been, track your current spending patterns against your budget. If you don't already have it included in your budget, make regular contributions to savings. For at least three months, track everything you earn and spend so you know where your money is coming from and where it is going.

At the end of each month do you have money left over? If so, you have a "positive cash flow." If you don't have that money "in hand" (not just on paper but in real spending money), or do not have enough to pay all your budgeted expenses, you are not in a position to buy a home, unless by doing so you are able to decrease your living expenses. Instead, you're kidding yourself and headed for trouble.

It is important for you to know how much extra you have to spend; if you buy a home, that amount is the maximum additional monthly expense you can afford without changing your spending habits. Do not be lured into a false sense of hope by assuming that your income will increase and you will be able to cover your expenses. Do not count on changing your spending habits after your buy your home. The time to change those habits is before you buy.

No matter how much money they make, some people will always spend all or more than they have. It is a way of operating around

Table 2-1. Monthly Budget

Payments Against Liabilities	
Mortgage Payment or Rent	
Real Estate Taxes	
Interest on Mortgage	
Vacation Home Mortgage	
Personal Property Taxes	
Auto Loan	
Personal Loans	
Charge Accounts	
Other	
Total Payments Against Liabilities	
Income Taxes	
Federal	
State	
Local	
Medicare	
Total Taxes	
Utilities	
Electricity	
Heat	
Water	
Air Conditioning	
Cable	
Telephone	
Other	
Total Utilities	
Transportation	
Gas & Oil	
Maint. & Repair	
License	
Public Transportation	
Parking	
Total Transportation	
Income Sources	
Your Salary	
Your Social Security	
Your Other	
Spouse Salary	
Spouse Social Security	
Spouse Other	
Investment Income	
Other Income	
TOTAL INCOME	
TOTAL EXPENSES	
Discretionary Income	

Insurance	
Life	
Health	
Dental	
Disability Income	
Auto	
Home Owner's	
Other	
Total Insurance	
Savings & Investments	
Payroll Deductions	
Credit Union	
Mutual Funds	
Stocks & Bonds	
Real Estate	
Annuities	
Face Amount Certificates	
Other	
Total Savings & Investments	
Contributions	
Religious	
Charitable	
Total Contributions	
Household Expenses	
Food	
Clothing	
Doctor (Including Eye Care)	
Dentist	
Prescription Drugs	
Personal Care	
Garbage	
Maintenance & Repair	
Home Furnishings	
Recreation, Entertainment, Hobbies	
Vacation & Travel	
Children Allowances	
Gifts	
Education (tuition, books, fees)	
Child Care	
Child Support	
Internet Access	
Lawn Care/Snow Removal	
Pest Control	
Miscellaneous	
Other	
Other	
Total Household Expenses	

finances that has nothing to do with how much they earn. We've known a successful executive for many years, who after each promotion and sizable salary increase, complained about always being "$136 short" at the end of the month. She was "$136 short" each month when she was earning $60,000 and "$136 short" when she was earning $185,000. She has a particular way of operating around money that creates this perpetual shortfall.

What is your way of operating around money? Monitoring your budget will help you to understand your way of operating. Until you have a clear and accurate picture of your spending habits and needs, you will not be able to determine how much you can spend on a home. Your mortgage payment is only a part of the expense of home ownership, and you will add these additional expenses to your current budget to determine what you can comfortably afford.

How a Lender Sees Your Finances

A lender looks at aspects of your budget through your loan application. When you complete a mortgage application, you supply information about your monthly rent and how much you pay per month for renter's insurance. You also state your monthly income, separating your base wages from overtime, commissions, bonuses, dividends, and other income.

To qualify for a *conforming loan,* a mortgage that is in compliance with Fannie Mae or Freddie Mac guidelines, and the most favorable terms available, your housing ratio should not exceed 28 percent. As a renter, the housing expense you use to calculate the housing ratio consists of rent and renter's insurance, but as a home owner it also includes real estate taxes, private mortgage insurance (if required), and association dues if your home is a condominium or co-op. If more than 28 percent of your gross income is going to be consumed by these housing expenses, you may not qualify for a loan, or you will pay more for the mortgage.

To know the maximum mortgage payment you can assume and retain a housing ratio of 28 percent or less, make the following calculation:

(Monthly income × .28) − (Taxes + Insurance) = Maximum mortgage payment

For example, if you earn $60,000 a year, your monthly income is $5,000. If you estimate taxes on a new house at $200 a month, and insurance of $100, your maximum recommended mortgage payment is calculated as follows:

Maximum mortgage payment = ($5,000 × .28) − ($200 + $100)
= ($1,400) − ($300)
= $1,100

In addition to the housing ratio, lenders compute your debt to income, or "back end" ratio, which includes your housing expenses and other loan and credit obligations. You will need a ratio of 36 percent or less to qualify for a conforming loan at the most favorable rates. The calculation for debt to income is:

(Housing expense + Minimum debt payments)/Income

Your minimum debt payments include car loans, student loans, other loans, and minimum payments on credit card and store charge card balances. These obligations should be included in your budget, but they also are included in your credit report, which becomes part of your loan application.

Using the earlier example, if you are earning $60,000 a year, and your taxes and insurance are going to be $300 a month, and monthly you pay $150 on a car loan and another $125 in minimum payments for credit card debt, then you can calculate the maximum mortgage payment that results in a debt to income ratio of 36 percent as follows:

Maximum mortgage payment = (Income × .36) − (Housing expense
+ Debt payments)
= ($5,000 × .36) − ($300 + $275)
= ($1,800) − ($575)
= $1,225

Take Advantage of Prequalification and Preapproval Services

Knowing the maximum mortgage payment that will qualify you for the best loans is useful in estimating the amount of money you can borrow, but that amount will fluctuate with interest rates. How do you know the right price range for homes for which you will be able to obtain good financing? Everyone shopping for their first home has the same question. Lenders provide two services that can assist you: prequalification and preapproval.

A *prequalification* letter from a lender states that based on information you provided, you are credit worthy. *Preapproval* is a more formal and thorough process whereby, based on complete loan application information, the lender commits to lend you a certain sum of money at a certain rate, assuming that the property you purchase fits specified parameters, the most significant being price. Armed with a preapproval, you can shop for homes within the preapproved range with a high degree of certainty that you will obtain financing when you find the home of your dreams. Sellers find preapproved buyers attractive because they know that financing will not become an obstacle to completing the sale.

Know the True Cost of Home Ownership

Just because a lender preapproves you for a mortgage for a home of a certain value does not mean you can afford it. Lenders' standards are designed to protect them. It is your job to protect you. If you have never owned or purchased a home, you may be surprised by the things for which you have to pay. It is up to you to plug the numbers for your new expenses into your budget and see the impact on your monthly bottom line. Be honest with yourself as to whether you can live within the adjusted budget now, not when you get your next salary increase or when you give up your daily lattes and weekly dinners out. Can you afford a home now, from the get-go?

When you buy a home and take a mortgage, you incur lots of costs. You pay costs related to the mortgage process and settlement with the seller, one-time expenses for items you need in and around your home, new monthly expenses, and occasional costs associated with maintaining your home.

Down Payment

As explained in Chapter 1, the value of your home is security for the lender should you default in your payments. To get the best mortgage pricing, your loan amount should not exceed 80 percent of the value of your home. This means that you need a down payment of at least 20 percent of your home's value to qualify for the most favorable terms. If you borrow more than 80 percent, the lender may require that you pay PMI with your monthly mortgage payment. The greater the percentage of the purchase price you borrow, the more PMI you will pay, and the longer you will pay it. Avoid paying PMI if you can, but don't sink every last dime of savings into your down payment; leave yourself a cushion for emergencies and for peace of mind.

100 Percent Financing. You can buy a home with little or no down payment. Some lenders will finance 100 percent of the purchase price of your new home (some even more, to cover closing costs). Sometimes lenders that are willing to finance 100 percent of your home's value will offer you two mortgages instead of one. The first mortgage for 80 percent of the value avoids the PMI requirement. A second mortgage for 20 percent is likely to be at a higher rate of interest, but the interest is tax-deductible, whereas the cost of PMI is not.

If you qualify for 100 percent or more financing, think twice before putting yourself into this high-risk situation. Again, qualifying for a loan doesn't always mean you can afford it. Be honest with yourself about why you don't have enough savings to put some money down. If you are unable to save, whatever the reason, you are in dangerous territory when you finance 100 percent of your home. If interest rates on an ARM rise or taxes or insurance rates increase, or the price of gasoline or heating oil rise significantly, you could be unable to meet your monthly expenses, and ultimately unable to pay your mortgage. And if real estate values decline, you may be unable to sell your home at a price that will cover all the outstanding debt.

Local, State, and Federal Down Payment Assistance. If you have never owned a home, you may qualify for first-time home-buyer programs offered by the federal Housing and Urban Development agency (HUD). The Federal Housing Authority (FHA) within HUD insures mortgages for first-time home buyers. Displaced homemakers and people who have not owned a home in three years may also qualify for FHA programs. FHA-insured loans relax the down payment percentage requirement, by requiring as little as 3 percent down.

Your state and local government and local nonprofits may also offer down-payment assistance programs. Some state housing finance authorities or agencies provide grants and low- or no-interest loans to first-time home buyers and others who need assistance to buy a home. The National Council of State Housing Agencies (NCSHA) has a website at www.ncsha.org where you can find contact information for housing agencies in your state. Check with your state's agency to learn about programs, and qualification and residency requirements.

And, if you qualify as a first-time home buyer, you may be able to withdraw up to $10,000 (or up to $20,000 for some couples) early from an IRA without penalty for a down payment. Check IRS Publication 590 (at www.irs.gov) for specific terms and conditions.

Costs Related to Financing

In addition to the down payment, you will pay other costs associated with obtaining a mortgage. These may include a loan application fee, appraisal fee, credit report fee, inspection fees, title insurance, filing fees, wire transfer fees, attorney fees, and a host of other "closing costs." You may have to pay the seller a portion of the annual expenses for items such as property taxes and heating oil, prorated for the timing of your closing. Your *closing settlement statement*, a legally required document prepared by an attorney or settlement agent, itemizes these expenses. You will be required to pay these expenses out-of-pocket, or add them to the amount you borrow.

One-Time Costs

Moving can be an expensive proposition. If you are unable to pack and transport your belongings yourself, you will have to pay someone else to move you. If you can't live with the shaggy brown carpet and orange flowered wallpaper the previous owners left, plan to spend money to ready the house for your arrival.

If you've been renting, you may not own your refrigerator, stove, washer, dryer, or microwave. Don't assume these things come with the house you are buying. Don't assume that light fixtures, window treatments (such as shades or blinds), or statuaries are included, either. These items are negotiable, and if they are not included be prepared to have to buy them. If you are not certain, ask. If the cost of such items is not included in the purchase price of your home, you can include the estimated cost in the amount you finance. Remember, however, that for every dollar you add to the amount you are borrowing, you are increasing the monthly payment and increasing the total amount of interest you are paying.

If your new home has a yard and lawn, be prepared to spend money on a lawn mower, trimmer, hoses, rakes, tools, a wheelbarrow, dirt, mulch, plants, and lawn treatments. If you live in a climate with a snowy winter, add snow shovels or blowers to your list of necessary equipment. Your alternative to these sizable one-time expenditures is to hire people to provide lawn care and snow removal services for you, and factor these recurring expenses into your monthly budget.

New Monthly Expenses

Real estate taxes are a part of home ownership. They vary tremendously from one city to another, and even cities within the same state can have very different tax rates. Your lender may require you to pay a portion of your estimated real estate taxes each month in addition to your principal and interest. The lender or other mortgage servicer holds the amount you pay monthly in an "escrow" account and pays the tax bill when due.

Lenders also require that you pay for *homeowner's insurance,* and specify the minimum amount of coverage you must carry. Insurance rates vary by provider and amount of coverage. Not to be confused with PMI, this insurance protects you against damage to your home.

As a home owner you may have to pay for services that you take for granted as a renter, such as garbage removal, pest control, snow-plowing, and water and sewer connections. Utilities such as heat, air conditioning, and electricity may be substantially higher in a house than in an apartment. Those vaulted ceilings and picture windows you fell in love with could cost you plenty in higher heating or electric bills. Ask the seller about the annual cost of taxes, insurance, assessments, heating, air conditioning, electricity, and services and adjust your monthly budget accordingly. Once you add in these items into your current budget, you will start to have a sense of whether you can afford your home and the changes you will have to make (or not) in order to do so.

Maintenance

When you rent, maintenance of your living space and its major systems is almost always the responsibility of the landlord. When you own your own home, you enter the world of owning things such as furnaces, hot water tanks, oil tanks, water treatment systems, septic systems, air conditioning systems, and wells. Exterior maintenance for the roof, gutters, driveway, and exterior walls or siding all add to the cost of home ownership. Plumbing, electrical, and appliance repairs are your responsibility as well. Although these are not regular monthly expenses, you should know what the annual service and maintenance costs are and plan accordingly when deciding how much home you can afford.

An inspection report prior to closing should identify problem areas in advance so you can negotiate for the seller to handle repairs before closing, or negotiate an allowance to compensate you for the cost of needed repairs. The inspection also tells you the age and condition of the major systems and the roof, so you can anticipate the timing of needed replacements and budget accordingly. In addition, the inspection will alert you to environmental issues that could cost you a lot of money to eliminate or protect against, including the presence of lead, asbestos, radon, inground oil tanks, and flooding. Unless you put money aside each month to cover the costs of maintenance and repairs when they arise, you can find yourself distressed and facing substantial additional debt to take care of your home.

Navigating the Mortgage Minefield: Don't Stretch

We have worked with some great realtors. Good ones are as interested in your financial well-being as they are in making the sale. They listen to you about the price range and attributes you seek in a home, and show only properties that fit the parameters. Other realtors push buyers to look at homes above the high end of the range they state. Don't fall for it. If you set a range, stick to it, or you will be looking at homes you cannot afford. It is very difficult to resist that urge to stretch yourself financially when you are standing in a house that you love and which is beyond your means. Don't put yourself in that position. Politely decline viewing houses outside your range, and save yourself the disappointment of wanting what you cannot have, or the anxiety of buying what you cannot afford. If the realtor continues to show you homes outside your range, change realtors. There are plenty of good ones out there.

Be honest with yourself about your spending habits and the likelihood of "tightening your belt" to afford a home. What impact will it have on you and your family? Are you really going to forego vacations, or will you increase your debt to "have it all"? Think about how you react to and deal with stress before you take up a heavy financial load.

If you use the suggestions in this chapter to determine for yourself how much you can afford to spend on a home, you will make a smart decision, and you will be able to enjoy your home without financial concern. That is, after all, what it is all about.

KNOW HOW MUCH YOUR PROPERTY IS WORTH

The value of the property for which you are obtaining a mortgage is one of the biggest factors in determining how much money you will be able to borrow. Lenders want a cushion between what you borrow and the value of the property so that if you default they will be able to sell your home and recover the amount you owe. For this reason, lenders look for a loan to value ratio of no more than 80 percent. How do you know how much your property is worth? In this chapter you will learn:

☑ How to differentiate between the price of a home and its market value

☑ How an appraisal affects the amount you can borrow, and what you can do about it

☑ Why a home inspection can be beneficial and how the conditions of a property can reduce its value now or in the future

☑ What factors can affect the future value of your home

Distinguishing Between the Price of a Home and Its Value

In a perfectly balanced real estate market, where the supply of houses for sale is perfectly matched to the demand from buyers, the price of a home would match its value. In reality, there are a number of factors that affect not only the real estate market but the determination of a home's value for the purposes of securing a mortgage.

Let's be clear that what you as a buyer value in a home may have nothing to do with its valuation for the purposes of an appraisal and a loan. Presumably, if you have found a home you want to buy, there are features about it that you like, but the crown molding and abundant closet space you so admire have little impact on an appraiser's valuation of the property. And don't forget that a wood-surrounded home at the end of a cul-de-sac that is "very private" to one person may seem "too isolated" to another. These features may not figure into the value of the home, but depending on the market, the neighborhood and popular trends and fashions may have a lot to do with the price the seller is asking.

A seller who uses a real estate broker or agent may rely on that professional to provide a *comparative market analysis (CMA)* to guide the initial asking price for the property. A CMA is an analysis of recent real estate transactions in your area. It provides data about homes currently on the market, about homes that are under sale contract, recent completed sales, and homes that were for sale but were taken off the market. The CMA also compares your property to others in your area that are of comparable style, age, condition, and location. Real estate professionals sometimes offer CMAs at no charge to attract home owners to the seller's market. If you are considering refinancing your home and want a ballpark estimate of its value without the expense of an appraisal, a CMA, offered by a good professional, could give you an estimate that is close to the appraised value. It is important to understand, however, that the CMA is based primarily on the asking prices of other homes that are being actively marketed at the same time, and it is not a recognized valuation of the property for purposes of obtaining a mortgage.

How Value Is Determined for Purposes of a Mortgage

Ultimately, what you pay for your home is your business. When you apply for a mortgage, the value of your home becomes the lender's business and determines whether the amount you will be able to borrow is sufficient to pay the seller's asking price. Lenders rely on the skills and experience of licensed appraisers to determine the value of the property for which a mortgage is being applied.

Appraisers are licensed in each state to perform an objective analysis of a home's surrounding, attributes, condition, and the prevailing local real estate market to estimate the market value of the property. The appraiser visits the property to document its size, number of rooms, and condition, and also researches town land records for land use and zoning restrictions, and analyzes recent sales of comparable homes in the neighborhood to arrive at an estimated market value for the property. Appraisers report their findings on a Uniform Residential Appraisal Report, which is an industry-standard checklist and form that facilitates comparison of the characteristics of properties that affect their values.

Neighborhood. The appraiser reports on characteristics and trends in the neighborhood that make it more or less desirable and that could affect the value of the property in the future. The fact that a neighborhood is urban, suburban, or rural is noted. This designation is predominantly an indication of the density of development in the area. Along with other factors, such as zoning restrictions, it indicates how much future development is possible, which could change the nature of the neighborhood. An urban neighborhood is not likely to transform into a rural one, but a rural area, barring zoning and land use restrictions to prevent it, could become suburban or even urban in character over time. The appraiser indicates the degree to which the area is built up, how fast it is growing, and whether the trend in property values is increasing, stable, or declining.

In addition to these longer-term neighborhood indicators, the appraiser uses information about recent sales of other homes in the neighborhood to report whether supply and demand in the local market are balanced, and the average time homes for sale remain on the market. General real estate market conditions, including mortgage rates, are also reported. Additionally, the appraiser notes features of the neighborhood that make it attractive to buyers, such as its proximity to shopping, schools, recreation, and employment centers.

The appraiser reports the high and low property values in the neighborhood, and the general condition of other homes. As a buyer, if your home is the most expensive in the neighborhood, you will likely pay less than you would for the same house in a better neighborhood, as the surrounding properties lower the value of the home. If you are selling and your home is the most expensive in your neighborhood, you may not get as high a price as the same home in a more expensive neighborhood. Similarly, as a buyer, if your home is the least expensive in the neighborhood you may pay more than you would for the same home in a less expensive neighborhood. On the other hand, as the seller of the least expensive home in a neighborhood, you may be able to get a higher price based on the surrounding homes than you would if the same home were in a less expensive neighborhood. The appraiser reports whether the other properties in the neighborhood are used predominantly for single-family, multiunit, or commercial use, and the likelihood that the use of land will change in the future. All these neighborhood characteristics give the lender a sense of the current marketability and possible changes that could affect value in the future.

Features of Your Home That Affect Value. The "Site" section of the Uniform Residential Appraisal Report contains information about the lot of land and the supply of utilities. The appraiser indicates the size and shape of the lot and how the size and view from the property compare to others in the neighborhood.

One characteristic that could cost you money is the location of the property in a flood zone. The Federal Emergency Management Agency (FEMA) maintains maps for all parts of the country, and these maps designate flood hazard zones for each area. The appraisal report references the FEMA map number and the date the map was last updated by FEMA, and reports whether the property is in a FEMA designated Special Flood Hazard Zone. If it is, the lender will require you to carry flood insurance, which can run into several thousands of dollars and can increase your monthly housing expense by hundreds.

While most homes are supplied with electricity through public utilities, there are still parts of the country where gas, water, and sewage are privately managed with propane, wells, and septic systems, respectively. If nonpublic provision of these basic services is the neighborhood norm, the appraiser notes that the presence of these systems is not detrimental to the property value.

Any adverse conditions on the lot, such as easements, encroachments, or environmental conditions, are recorded in the appraisal. An *easement* allows someone else the legal right to use your property for a specific purpose, usually to access their property. A shared driveway is a common easement, and is somewhat detrimental to the value of the home because it potentially places restrictions on the changes you can make to the property. An *encroachment* is an overlap of property onto an adjacent property, such as a neighbor's fence that is technically on your land. Encroachments can complicate title issues, so it is best to avoid them if you can.

Navigating the Mortgage Minefield: Be Aware of How Your Neighborhood Could Change

An appraisal identifies the features of your property that affect its value, but the properties immediately surrounding yours also impact its salability, and you may have little or no control over changes that could alter the neighborhood and the attractiveness of your home to other buyers, should you want to sell. Unless you are aware of your surroundings, you could be caught by surprise if things change.

A friend of ours purchased a lovely home in a very private setting, at the end of a cul-de-sac off another cul-de-sac. There was no traffic other than from the two other families who lived on the street, making it very safe for children and pets to be outdoors. The lot next door was not suitable for building, assuring the distance between our friend and her closest neighbor. Behind the house was an undeveloped wooded ridge that extended as far as you could see, adding to the privacy and natural beauty of the location.

Several years after moving in, our friend received notice of a town hearing related to the development of houses along that beautiful ridge. That land had been privately owned, and upon the owner's death, had been sold to a real estate developer who was building seventeen million-dollar homes. The developers were considering building a road from the cul-de-sac to the new development, and our friend's first reaction was "They can't do that." Upon research, however, it turned out that they could: The cul-de-sac was officially designated "temporary" in the town records, meaning a through-road could be approved and built at any time, and it could come within ten feet of her driveway.

Fortunately for our friend, the developer decided not to put the road in, and the ridge remained wooded enough to retain her privacy. But the lesson was learned to know about the property surrounding yours, and not to make assumptions that it will always remain the same.

The "Improvements" section of the appraisal report notes the number and type of rooms on each level of the home as well as major appliances, such as refrigerator, oven, and dishwasher. It describes the building materials and condition of exterior surfaces such as the roof, gutters, siding, and windows, and of interior floors, walls, trim, and bathroom. Any repairs needed or obvious obsolescence is noted. Features and amenities of note such as central air conditioning, fireplace, patio or deck, garage, pool, fence, and attic add value to the home.

Obvious evidence of dampness, settlement disturbances, or pest infestations is noted. The appraiser looks for and notes the presence or absence of environmental conditions that could affect the property value, such as mold, asbestos, hazardous materials on or near the property, or the presence of inground heating-oil storage tanks. If evident, these things will be reported on the appraisal, but you should be aware that the appraiser is not performing an inspection that would specifically search out these conditions.

Comparison of Your Property to Others Recently Sold. As part of the appraisal, the appraiser researches and reports on homes in the neighborhood that recently have been sold and that are of similar style, age, and condition in order to estimate the market value of your home. The analysis lists side by side all the major features of your home with features of the other homes selected for the comparison, and adjusts the sales prices for differences that the appraiser considers material.

On the basis of all this information, the appraiser estimates the current market value of your home. The lender uses that figure as the value of your property to calculate your loan to value ratio, and ultimately, how much you will be able to borrow.

What Happens If the Appraisal Is Too Low for the Loan Amount?

If the appraised value of the property varies significantly from the asking price, consider very carefully what is affecting the valuation and the seller's price. If the home is in a highly desirable neighborhood and homes are in short supply compared to the number of interested buyers, the selling price of a home may exceed its value. In this case, you may have to make a larger down payment in order to remain within the LTV guideline of 80 percent. If your LTV is more than 80 percent, the lender may raise your interest rate, charge more points, or require PMI.

If, on the other hand, the current owner must sell quickly, perhaps as a result of a job relocation or divorce, the asking price for the home may be below its value, in the hope of attracting interest and making a quick sale. In this case you may be able to borrow less, resulting in a lower LTV, and possibly reducing your interest rate.

Be aware that if there is a long period between the mortgage approval and your closing, the lender may have the right to a second appraisal right before closing. In markets where real estate prices are falling rapidly, the second appraisal may be lower than the purchase price of the home. Read the fine print of your loan approval and your purchase contract to know whether this could happen to you.

If you are purchasing a home and the appraisal value is too low for the amount of the loan you need, you have several options. You can negotiate with the seller for a lower price. If a seller relied on a real estate agent's CMA to set an asking price, that number could be unrealistic. Sometimes sellers base their initial sales price on emotion and hopefulness rather than market conditions and appraisal values. Or, it could be that conditions changed since the property was placed on the market; more houses are now for sale, or financing may be more difficult to obtain.

If you cannot negotiate a lower price, consider a larger down payment to bring the LTV ratio below 80 percent. If you are able to do that, you can avoid PMI and may be able to obtain a lower interest rate. If a larger down payment is not possible, you may still be able to get financing, although it may cost you a bit more in terms of a higher interest rate, or points at closing, and you may have to pay PMI.

Finally, you can challenge the appraisal. There may be features of the home such as marble counters or other high-quality materials that may have been overlooked, and which add value. If you believe that the comparable properties are not fully comparable, or that the recent sales are not typical for present market conditions, you can work with a realtor to suggest other properties and sales for the appraiser to consider. If not, you can request and pay for a second opinion from another appraiser.

The Value of a Home Inspection

An appraisal is not an inspection of the home. The appraisal benefits and protects the lender. A home inspection protects and benefits you, the buyer. If you are purchasing a home, in addition to the appraisal, which the lender requires, it is to your advantage to have the home professionally inspected before the purchase. You are responsible for obtaining and understanding the financial implications of the inspection report and will, most likely, also have to pay for the inspection. The money you spend on an inspection before you buy the house can save you thousands of dollars in repairs and replacements, so it is well worth the time and the cost.

When you make an offer to buy, it is common to include, as a condition of the sale, a satisfactory inspection report. If the report reveals significant structural or repair issues, this condition of sale gives you leverage with the seller. If there are major costs anticipated for the near future, you can negotiate an allowance, in the form of a reduction in price, from the seller. Put that savings aside and factor into your budget the additional money you will have to save to pay for the repairs and replacements in the future. Having the sale be conditional on a satisfactory inspection report allows you to cancel your offer if you cannot negotiate a satisfactory reduction in price or the handling of the repairs by the seller prior to closing.

Inspectors are licensed in some states. If your real estate agent or broker cannot recommend someone, the American Society of Housing Inspectors' website, www.ashi.org, can help you find an inspector in your area. The inspector visits the house and looks at the construction, the materials, and the age and condition of the major systems in the house, such as heating, plumbing, and electrical. Items needing replacement or repair are noted. The inspector also estimates the remaining life in the roof, furnace, air conditioning, and other major equipment, and looks for the presence of insect damage and mold, and other environmental conditions that need remediation.

Inspections for Specific Conditions That Could Affect the Value of Your Home

Inspection standards vary from state to state, so it is important that you know the conditions about which the inspector will report. If not included in the general inspection, you may choose to have the home inspected for one or more common conditions that can be very costly to correct, including asbestos, lead, radon, mold, and infestation by rodents, termites, and other uninvited guests.

Asbestos is sometimes found in older homes, and, if not maintained properly, can cause serious health risks, including cancer. If asbestos is present, it may not be necessary to remove it, but rather it can be encapsulated. Learn more at the Environmental Protection Agency website, www.epa.gov/asbestos.

Lead-based paint was outlawed in 1978, but homes built prior to that time may contain lead. Exposure to lead causes serious health issues, particularly among children. If your home was built before 1978, an inspection for the presence of lead can prepare you to take removal or other contamination prevention measures.

Radon is a naturally occurring radioactive gas that, when present in large concentrations, can cause serious health damage, including cancer. Radon testing has become routine, and self-testing kits are available at a discount from the National Safety Council. To learn more about radon, radon testing, and mitigation, start with www.epa .gov/radon, the Environmental Protection Agency's consumer awareness page.

Mold, mildew, and fungi can be annoyances, and may aggravate allergies or cause health problems. They thrive in damp conditions, and their presence may indicate serious structural problems or previous water damage from floods, plumbing, or roofing leaks. If they are found, inquire about their cause and what corrective actions have been taken. You may choose to have the air tested for invisible mold spores, particularly if you or a member of your household suffers from asthma or allergies.

Rodents, termites, and other unwanted animals that take up residence in your home can be a problem as well, as they can cause structural and health damage. The pests themselves can be eliminated by engaging an exterminator or other pest control specialist. If there is evidence of termites, carpenter ants, or other wood-eating insects, you should have the damaged areas inspected for structural damage, and make or negotiate appropriate repairs.

Self-Assessment for Refinancing

If you already own a home and are considering refinancing, you may be asking "what does this have to do with me?" This is the perfect time for you to take stock of your home, anticipate major repairs and replacements, and adjust your budget accordingly, before you decide what refinancing option is best for you. While you may not choose to hire a professional inspector, you should know whether your furnace is living on borrowed time, or whether the exterior is going to need a coat of paint in the next year or two. Before you make a refinancing decision, take stock of the condition of your home and what it will take financially to keep it functioning and marketable. Armed with that information, you can make an intelligent and informed decision about the refinancing options available to you.

Navigating the Mortgage Minefield: Land Use Restrictions That Affect the Value of Your Property

Most towns have zoning regulations that determine standards for the use and improvement of residential real estate. Often these regulations specify the distance between structures and surrounding property, the amount of footage on the street side that is required for a home to be built, the height of structures, and other items. If your home is in a historic district, there may even be regulations regarding what color you can paint the exterior of your home. What this means is that if you are planning to build out or build up you must be certain that there are no restrictions that would prevent you from doing so, or that would unduly limit your choices.

The deed to your property contains detailed information regarding boundaries and restrictions on land use. Read it. Remember our friend with the development going up behind her secluded home? Had she read the deed to her property, she would have known that the town had a right to construct a street bordering her property. You may be surprised to learn that your neighbor has a right to cross your property or share your driveway. Such easements are not a big deal, and do not give others a claim to the ownership of your property, but they do give others the right to specific usage of your property, which may limit the changes you can make.

Some parcels of real estate come with deed restrictions that specify and limit the way the property can be used or the types of structures that can be erected. Before you get your hopes set on building that storage shed or pool house, know whether such restrictions apply to your property.

Factors That Can Affect Future Property Value

Everyone who invests in real estate wants assurance that the value of the property will increase over time. Whether your home appreciates in value between the time you buy it and the time you want to sell it is influenced by general social and economic conditions, local market conditions, and factors that are specific to your home. Some of the factors that affect the future value of your home, such as inflation and mortgage interest rates, are things over which you have absolutely no say or influence. Other factors are within your control. While it is impossible to predict with certainty whether or by how much your property will appreciate, you can gain insight into the likelihood of the value of your property increasing.

Economic Influences

One of the major economic factors that causes a rise in property value is *inflation*. Inflation results when the supply of money increases, causing the value of money to decline. In an inflationary period, general price levels rise, and the result is that what your dollar could buy before inflation will cost you more than a dollar after inflation. This is good for real estate values if you are selling your home, but not so good if you are buying.

Interest rates for mortgages also have an impact on property values. As interest rates rise, fewer people seek housing, causing the demand for property, and the price, to drop. When interest rates for mortgages are low and guidelines less restrictive, the demand for real estate rises and prices rise along with it.

One of the major economic factors in play today is a result of the collapse of the subprime lending market. This collapse has had a "double whammy" impact; the rise in foreclosures has resulted in a rapid growth in the supply of houses for sale, while the tightening lending markets have cut into the demand previously stoked by easy access to affordable mortgages. In reaction to negative publicity and rising defaults, lenders have made it more difficult for borrowers with good credit to obtain mortgages at the best rates.

Neighborhood Influences

Population increases in your city or neighborhood also affect real estate values. If more people are drawn to a particular area, especially where new housing development is limited, prices for real estate will rise. Population increases can result from new job availability or from nearby commercial development that improves proximity to shopping areas, schools, and similar services. Is your neighborhood or its surrounding area likely to undergo substantial commercial development? Are there large tracts of undeveloped commercially zoned land in the area? What is the local policy for attracting employers to the area?

Decreases in population and the resulting decline in property values can result from increased crime rates, loss of job opportunities, and general economic decline of a city or town. Look at the businesses in the center of town. Are there many vacancies, or do the businesses appear to be thriving? Do you feel safe on the streets? Is the rate of serious crimes increasing in your town or neighboring towns? Particularly in suburban areas that border urban centers, how is the metropolitan area faring? Are people attracted to it or fleeing from it?

Property tax rates can influence real estate prices as well. If the town you live in has a tax rate that is higher and rising faster than that of surrounding towns, property values in your town could decline relative to those in neighboring towns. The local town government can provide information on tax rate trends.

Personal Influences

While many factors that affect long-term appreciation of property value are not within your direct control, there are others that will influence the value of your home over which you have complete control. General maintenance is one such factor, and has a large bearing on how well your home keeps its value. Remember all those items listed in the appraisal report? Keep them in good working order, and keep their appearances clean and neat to retain their value. Keep the exterior of your home looking good and in good condition as well. Peeling paint, dry-rotted trim, and droopy gutters detract from the appeal of your home and can cost you money when you sell it.

Improvements to your home can raise the value of your property. A remodeled kitchen or bath, when done at a reasonable cost, can return its cost to you in an increased value of your home. Additions of bedrooms, bathrooms, or storage can also make a home more appealing to potential buyers and can result in a higher appraisal. New carpeting, doors, windows, siding, roof, major appliances, and equipment such as energy-efficient heating and air conditioning can all increase the value of your home.

If you do not maintain your home properly, you may see any increases in property value due to economic and neighborhood conditions disappear as givebacks to the buyer to compensate for needed repairs, or as fewer or lower offers on your property. Your ability to maintain your home to retain and increase its value is a function of your budget, which brings us right back to your mortgage. Remember that the lender's guideline for an 80 percent LTV is based on having a cushion between the amount of money you borrow and the value of the home in case you default and the lender has to sell the home to recover the money you owe. Your job is to do everything in your power to maintain and improve the value of your home, and not to default on the mortgage. Being realistic about and budgeting for the maintenance and repair costs for your home are a first step toward meeting both these goals.

CHAPTER 4

WEIGH YOUR REFINANCING OPPORTUNITIES

The process for refinancing a home is almost the same as obtaining financing when you purchase a home. It begins with a mortgage application and goes through the same underwriting process as any other mortgage. Factors that are important to a lender when you purchase a home are also important when you refinance a home: Will you be able to make the payments, and will the value of the home cover the outstanding debt if you default on those payments?

When you refinance a home, you pay off your existing mortgage and take on a new one. You may get your new mortgage from your original lender, or from a new lender. Since many lenders sell their loans, you may no longer be a customer of the lender with whom you first did business, and they may have no incentive to provide you with better-than-market offers that you might expect from being an existing customer.

At the new mortgage closing, you pay the balance of the old mortgage with funds from the new mortgage. The original lender releases its lien against your property, and the new lender files a lien to secure its interest.

Refinancing your home can be a smart financial decision; it can be a way to improve your cash flow, eliminate other debt, or finance major expenses or investments. However, it can also be a self-defeating practice that supports bad financial habits by enabling a debt-refinance debt cycle. Once again, before making a refinancing decision, it is important to be honest with yourself regarding the way you operate with respect to your finances. It is also important to be aware of the benefits and the risks of various refinancing options, and to understand both the short-term and long-term implications of your refinancing decisions. In this chapter, you will learn:

☑ Under what circumstances you should consider refinancing

☑ How refinancing can help you to improve your cash flow

☑ How refinancing can help you to fund major expenses

☑ How refinancing can help you to prepare for life-changing events

☑ How refinancing can help you to balance your short- and long-term financial needs

Why Refinance Your Home?

There are three main reasons to refinance your home. Refinancing can improve your cash flow, make large sums of money available to you to fund major purchases or investments, and improve your financial position to prepare for major life events such as retirement. Most people focus on the short-term effects of refinancing, such as lower monthly mortgage or debt payments, or money to spend on expenses like renovations, education, medical expenses, or vacations. But when you also understand the long-term effects of refinancing, you can better determine whether the terms of the refinance are right for you.

Refinance to Improve Your Cash Flow

When interest rates are declining as was the case during the mortgage boom that started around 2002, you are able to refinance your mortgage to take advantage of lower monthly mortgage payments that result from the lower rates. This can free up cash for other expenses, to balance your budget, or to put money away as savings.

When you refinance, you have choices to make not only regarding the interest rate, but also regarding the amount of principal, the loan term, and the closing costs you will incur. When you are aware of all the factors that may affect the cost of your mortgage, you can make an informed and responsible decision that meets your short-term goals and allows you to be aware of the long-term implications of your choices.

Isolating the Effect of Rate on Monthly Payments. The original terms of a thirty-year mortgage for $150,000 at 6.5 percent interest result in a total interest payment of $191,318.01 if you hold the mortgage for its full term. After fifteen years of monthly payments on this mortgage, you will have paid $129,497.24 in interest and your principal balance will be $108,839.24.

Table 4-1 compares continuation of the original thirty-year mortgage for the remaining fifteen years with a refinance option at a lower rate of interest for fifteen years. In each case, the starting principal balance is the $108,839.24 still owed, and no balance remains at the end of fifteen additional years. As you can see, the monthly payment drops from $948.10 to $889.31, a savings of $58.79 per month. If you put that savings aside in a cookie jar each month, after fifteen years you will have accumulated $10,582.20. Put that money each

Table 4-1. Effect of Rate Reduction

	Original 30-year Fixed	15 Years of Remaining Payments	15-year Refinance
Principal	$150,000	$108,839	$108,839
Interest rate	6.50%	6.50%	5.500%
Monthly payment	$948.10	$948.10	$889.31
Total interest to pay	$191,318.01	$191,318.01	$51,235.53
Principal balance after 15 years	$108,839.24	$0.00	$0.00
Interest paid	$129,497.24	$61,820.77	$51,235.53
Cumulative interest paid	$129,497.24	$191,318.01	$180,732.77
Total savings		$0.00	$10,585.24

month into a savings account earning 2 percent interest and you will accumulate an additional $1,602 in savings.

Isolating the Effect of Extending Term. Refinancing your remaining mortgage balance at a lower rate of interest can lower the amount of interest you pay over the life of the loan, assuming you do not substantially extend the term of the loan. For example, Table 4-2 shows the same original thirty-year mortgage after fifteen years, and indicates the cost of extending the remaining term of the mortgage to thirty years.

Even without reducing the interest rate, the resulting monthly payment is substantially lower, dropping from $948.10 to $687.94 for a savings of $260.16 per month, purely as a result of extending the term. For most people, an extra $260.16 a month is a noticeable amount; it could cover an automobile payment, an insurance bill, or a heating bill for a month. Are you going to save that money? Or are you likely to use it to pay bills or better your standard of living?

If you are stretching to pay your bills every month, extending the term of your mortgage can seem like an attractive option that will

Table 4-2. Effect of Extending Term

	Original 30-year Fixed	15 Years of Remaining Payments	30-year Refinance	At the End of the Original 30 Years
Principal	$150,000	$108,839	$108,839	$108,839
Interest rate	6.50%	6.50%	6.500%	6.500%
Monthly payment	$948.10	$948.10	$687.94	$687.94
Total interest to pay	$191,318.01	$191,318.01	$138,815.38	$138,815.38
Principal balance after 15 years	$108,839.24	$0.00	$0.00	$78,971.50
Interest paid	$129,497.24	$61,820.77	$138,815.38	$93,961.70
Cumulative interest paid	$129,497.24	$191,318.01	$268,312.62	$155,782.47
Total savings		$0.00	($76,994.61)	$35,535.54

ease your month-to-month struggle. But you must understand that you are, in effect, borrowing against the equity in your home each month that you extend the term of your financing, and that it will cost you significantly more in the long term.

At the end of the second loan, the cumulative interest paid between the two loans is $268,312.62, which is $76,994.61 more than the "do nothing" option to complete the term of the original thirty-year mortgage. Even if you saved that $260.16 per month for the first fifteen years of the refinance, at 2 percent interest you would have about $54,616 accumulated, which would cover only about six and a half years of the remaining fifteen years of monthly payments.

At the end of the first thirty years (or fifteen years into the new thirty-year mortgage), when the original mortgage would have been paid in full, you are worse off than you would be if you did nothing. You will have paid $35,535.54 less in interest to date, but you would have $78,971.50 remaining as a balance on the mortgage and another fifteen years of payments ahead of you.

Consolidating Debt to Improve Cash Flow. Refinancing can provide access to money to pay off loans, credit cards, and other debts, and reduce monthly cash outflow. By tapping into the equity in your home, you can increase the amount of principal you are borrowing, and use that money to pay down or pay off other debt. This strategy can result in a monthly payment for the larger mortgage that is lower than the current combined mortgage, loan, and credit card payments. But as with any refinancing decision, the short-term benefit of improved cash flow comes with a long-term cost.

Table 4-3 shows how refinancing with cash out to pay off other debt improves cash flow. Assuming the same thirty-year fixed-rate mortgage at 6.5 percent interest as in previous examples, add in a balance of $16,700 on a car loan with a monthly payment of $500.00

Table 4-3. Effect on Cash Flow of Debt Consolidation

	Mortgage	Car Loan	Credit Card	Totals	Cash Out
Original loan principal	$150,000.00	$26,500.00			
Balance	$108,839.24	$16,700.00	$5,000.00	$130,539.24	$21,700.00
Interest rate	6.50%	5.00%	13.00%		
Monthly payment	$948.10	$500.00	$125.00	$1,573.10	
Total interest due	$191,318.01	$3,505.26	$3,644.62	$198,467.89	
Interest paid to date	$129,497.24	$2,187.88	$0.00	$131,685.12	
Refinance	**Mortgage**	**Car Loan**	**Credit Card**	**Totals**	
Principal	$130,539.24	$0.00	$0.00		
Interest rate	6.50%				
Term	30				
Payment	$825.10	0	0	$825.10	
Total interest due	$166,495.61	0	0	$166,495.61	
Interest paid to date				$298,180.73	

and minimum credit card payments of $125.00 per month. Total cash outlay per month for these obligations is $1,573.10. If a thirty-year fixed-rate mortgage for $130,539 is taken at the same 6.5 percent interest, and the car loan and credit card balances are paid in full with the $21,700 above the amount needed to pay the balance of the original mortgage, the new monthly payment is only $825.10, a hefty savings of $748.00 per month.

Once again, the short-term savings come at a long-term cost. If you do not refinance, the total interest you will pay on all the debt is $198,467.89. If you refinance at the terms in the example, the total interest paid after all obligations are paid is the $131,685.12 paid to date, plus the $166,495.61 on the refinanced mortgage for a total of $298,180.73, an increase of almost $100,000.00.

Tax Savings from Mortgage Interest Deductions. In addition to the improvement in cash flow, debt consolidation through a refinance has tax benefits for those who meet certain requirements. If you itemize your deductions, the interest you pay on a mortgage is tax-deductible. Credit card and other kinds of loan interest are not tax-deductible. By reducing your gross taxable income by the amount of your mortgage interest, you lower your tax rate, and this has the effect of a lower interest rate on the mortgage. Using the previous example, assuming a 25 percent income tax rate, the effective after-tax interest rate on your 6.5 percent mortgage is 4.875 percent. This is an effective savings of over $48,000 over the life of the loan, partially offsetting the higher expense.

Navigating the Mortgage Minefield: Avoid the Debt-Refinance-Debt Cycle

We often help people refinance to get out from under crushing credit card debt. Unfortunately, we see some of the same people every few years; having gotten out of trouble once, their good intentions do not keep them out of trouble for long. They repeat the debt-refinance-debt cycle as long as real estate values and the mortgage markets permit.

Unless your credit card debt is the result of extraordinary one-time expenses such as catastrophic nonreimbursed medical bills, whatever got you into credit card debt in the first place is unlikely to go away. Running up credit card debt is a way of operating that you will repeat unless you are aware of it and make a conscious decision to change it. This requires that you be very honest with yourself. If you follow the budgeting tips in Chapter 2, then you will have put aside money for ordinary expenses, including most nonreimbursed medical. If you are not doing that, you are operating with money in a way that is likely to have you in debt to credit card companies again in a few years. Visit www.roadtoriches.com for programs that support you to change the way you operate with regard to your finances.

As long as real estate values are stable or climbing, you will be able to continue your debt-refinance-debt cycle and will be able to tap into the equity in your home every few years. And plenty of people will make a lot of money from your poor habits. If, however, real estate values decline, you will be in deep trouble. You may find that the equity in your home is not sufficient to bail you out of your credit card habit. Or you may find, as is the case in today's tightening markets, stricter credit, income, and LTV requirements prevent you from refinancing.

Refinance to Fund Major Expenses

The equity in your home is a potential source of funding for major expenses such as education, remodeling, or medical costs. You cannot depend on that equity to be there at the time you need it, however, as there are no guarantees that the value of your home will increase by the amount or within the time you need the funds. If you have sizable equity in your home, it provides a relatively low-cost way to pay for these major expenses over a long period, minimizing the short-term financial impact of these expenditures. You can turn the equity in your home into cash in several ways: refinancing your home for a larger principal amount than your current mortgage (cash out), taking a second mortgage (also known as a home equity loan), applying for a home equity line of credit, or using a reverse mortgage. Each of these financial products gives you access to the equity in your home, but each has features and conditions of which you should be aware before making your decision. And remember, there are no guarantees that real estate values will keep pace with your cash requirements, and should values drop, you could owe more on your mortgage than your home is worth.

Tapping into Equity: Refinance with Cash Out. The scenario of accessing equity to pay off debt in Table 4-3 shown earlier is an example of refinancing with "cash out." Instead of borrowing only the $108,839.24 needed to pay off the principal balance on the original mortgage, in that example the new mortgage has a starting principal amount of $130,539.24. The extra $21,700.00, (the "cash out" amount), used to pay the auto loan and credit card balances, came from the equity in the home. In that case, the use of equity improved cash flow.

You can also use your equity to fund major expenditures such as college tuition, vacations, or medical bills. You use the equity to avoid higher-interest rate credit and avoid an increase in your monthly bills, which is an indirect cash flow impact.

Equity is also a source for large sums of money for other investments, such as home improvements, business ventures, or down payments on investment properties. In the case of home improvements, you recoup part of the equity from the increase in your home's market value that the improvements provide. If you use the equity as a down payment for a leveraged investment or an income-producing investment, you can increase your net worth, and improve your cash flow.

Home Equity Loan (Second Mortgage). A *home equity loan,* also known as a second mortgage, is a separate mortgage in addition to your primary, or first, mortgage. It requires an application, appraisal, title search, underwriting, and closing costs, just as a first mortgage does. Interest paid on a second mortgage is tax-deductible, assuming you itemize your deductions on your tax return.

The security interest of the second-mortgage lender is subordinate to the security interest of the first-mortgage holder. This means that the second-mortgage lender cannot recover your debt until the first-mortgage lender has been paid. Due to the increased risk, interest rates on second mortgages tend to be higher than the prevailing rates for first mortgages at any point in time.

Why take a second mortgage instead of refinancing a first mortgage? It allows you to pay off the second mortgage over a different length of time than the first. If you are borrowing the money for a specific reason, and know that you will pay it back in less than the term remaining on your first mortgage, it makes sense to take a second mortgage. Or, if you don't have much time remaining on your first mortgage, and you need the second loan for a longer period, you can continue to pay off your first mortgage and borrow against the second without affecting your first. Remember, the shorter the time you take to repay the loan, the less interest you pay in total.

Home Equity Line of Credit. A *home equity line of credit (HELOC)* is a variation of a second mortgage. It allows you to tap into the equity as needed instead of in a lump sum. A home equity line of credit is a tremendous financial asset for people who have substantial equity in their homes, and who anticipate a change in circumstances that may affect their income or ability to meet their financial obligations for a short time.

For example, if you are considering a career change that may result in a temporary reduction in your income, a home equity line of credit can be a temporary safety net that enables you to meet your expenses, and you can borrow against the line of credit as you need it. If you are putting yourself or your children or grandchildren through college, a home equity line of credit allows you to borrow against your equity when tuition is due.

Home equity lines of credit usually come with adjustable rates of interest. Interest on HELOCs is tax-deductible assuming you itemize your deductions. Some lenders market HELOCs with enticingly low but temporary introductory rates, so, as with any adjustable rate loan, it's important to understand how, when, and by how much the interest rate can change before jumping in. HELOCs also are available with different pay-back options, including interest-only payments for a certain period before the principal is due. This flexibility makes HELOC payments attractive from a cash flow perspective. And since most HELOCs do not have prepayment penalties, you can eliminate the debt at any time.

Reverse Mortgage. If you are sixty-two years of age or older, you may qualify for a *reverse mortgage*, also known as a *Home Equity Conversion Mortgage*. With a regular mortgage and monthly payments that include principal and interest, assuming stable or rising market values, your equity increases with each payment you make to the lender. With a reverse mortgage, a lender pays you each month, in exchange for equity and interest that you pay to the lender when you sell your home or pass away. Each time you receive a payment, equity transfers from you to the lender.

For the elderly with substantial equity in their homes, a reverse mortgage provides a source of supplemental income that can significantly improve lifestyle and comfort. Terms for reverse mortgages are quite flexible, and can be tailored to suit the financial needs of the home owner. HUD guarantees some reverse mortgages and protects the lender in the event that the payments to the home owner exceed

the proceeds from the sale of the home. This protects the home owner's other assets in case the lender pays out more to the home owner
than the home is worth at the time of sale.

Refinance to Prepare for Life-Changing Events

Refinancing can be a powerful instrument for planning for future
life-changing events such as retirement or a career change. As you
have seen, you can use it to reduce cash outflow on a monthly basis,
eliminate or reduce other debt, and create access to large sums of
money when needed. A friend of ours was working as a manager in
a large corporation but wanted to start a business of her own. She
worked at both her job and the business for several years before deciding that she needed to focus her attention on the new business. Antic-
ipating that she would leave her job within six months to a year, she
refinanced to eliminate her automobile loan and reduced her monthly
payments by $1,200, put money into investment accounts to fund her
children's college tuition, and opened a HELOC to supplement her
income as needed once she quit her job, until the business could
generate enough profit to support her.

Weighing Short-Term Savings by Refinancing Against Long- and Short-Term Costs

Refinancing is a great tool for achieving short-term gratification and
relief from stress, and it is human nature to seek to have our immediate needs and wants met. If you are in sudden and urgent need of a
large sum of money or relief from overwhelming bills, the equity in
your home can seem like the only way to solve your immediate problem, and it may be. But that doesn't mean it is the smart thing to do.
As with any financial decision, you must consider the short- and long-
term implications to make a responsible and informed choice.

Unfortunately, if you find yourself with a financial emergency on your hands, you may be more preoccupied with the circumstances that caused the emergency than with the analysis of your borrowing options. Be careful. Do not, in your haste to seek immediate financial relief, commit to a loan that will get you into long-term financial trouble, or that may be difficult to get out of. I have seen people faced with medical crises who sign mortgage agreements without fully appreciating adjustment terms or prepayment penalties, and find themselves unable to meet their mortgage obligations and unable to refinance. Whatever circumstances require access to your equity, take the time to know and be responsible for what you are getting into. If you don't, you may find your troubles compounded rather than relieved.

The examples used earlier in this chapter demonstrated the effects of rate, term, and principal choices that are part of a refinancing decision. We used scenarios where there were fifteen years remaining on the original mortgage to make comparisons between thirty-year and fifteen-year refinancing options. In the previous examples, fifteen years of fixed-rate payments had been made, and because of the way repayment is amortized in mortgages, more than 63 percent of the interest due on the thirty-year loan had already been paid. The reality is that the average length of time a thirty-year mortgage is held before it is either refinanced or paid off through the sale of the home is between three and four years. Since the interest already paid is a major component of the long-term impact and overall cost of refinancing, the length of time you have been making payments is a determining factor in the financial analysis you should be doing. In the previous examples, at the end of fifteen years of a thirty-year fixed-rate mortgage for $150,000.00 at 6.5 percent, total interest paid was $129,497.08 of the $191,318.01, or 67.7 percent, that would be paid at the completion of the thirty-year term. Using the same example, at the end of four years the interest paid is $38,098.35, or 19.9 percent of the total interest due, and the balance is higher, at $142,589.45.

Table 4-4 compares the thirty-year and fifteen-year balance refinancing costs for the mortgage after fifteen years (top), with the mortgage after four years (bottom). In the first case the monthly payment drops from $948.10 to $643.82, while in the case of refinancing after four years, the monthly payment drops only to $843.47. The monthly payment reduction is smaller in the second case, because a larger principal balance ($142,589 compared to $108,839) remains to refi-

Table 4-4. Comparison of Refinance Options After 15 and 4 Years

	Original 30-year Fixed	30-year Refinance	15-year Refinance
Principal	$150,000	$108,839	$108,839
Interest rate	6.50%	5.875%	5.875%
Monthly payment	$948.10	$643.82	$911.11
Total interest to pay	$191,318.01	$122,939.95	$55,161.18
Number of years of payments	15	30	15
Principal balance	$108,839.24	$0.00	$0.00
Interest paid to date	$129,497.08	$252,437.03	$184,658.26
Total savings		($61,119.02)	$6,659.75
	Original 30-year Fixed	30-year Refinance	15-year Refinance
Principal	$150,000	$142,589	$142,589
Interest rate	6.50%	5.875%	5.875%
Monthly payment	$948.10	$843.47	$1,193.64
Total interest to pay	$191,318.01	$161,058.04	$72,265.90
Number of years of payments	4	30	15
Principal balance	$142,589.45	$0.00	$0.00
Interest paid to date	$38,098.25	$199,156.29	$110,364.15
Total savings		($7,838.28)	$80,953.86

nance. However, the long-term cost is substantially lower, as less interest was paid to date on the original mortgage. After fifteen years of payments, you will have paid $129,497.08 in interest, compared to only $38,098.25 after four years.

The comparison for the fifteen-year refinancing option is more dramatic. The monthly payment increases from $948.10 to $1,193.64, but the long-term savings of $80,952.58 is over 42 percent of the total interest that was due on the original mortgage.

In Table 4-2 we showed the effect of extending term by assuming equal interest rates for thirty-year refinancing and fifteen-year refinancing. When it comes time for you to refinance, rates for different mortgages will vary. Table 4-5 shows the type of choice you would typically face at the time of your refinancing decision.

Regardless of the rate for the thirty-year fixed, rates for fifteen-year fixed are typically .375 to .5 percent lower. In this example, refinancing a thirty-year fixed-rate mortgage after four years with a fifteen-year fixed-rate mortgage results in a savings of $86,095.88, or 45 percent of the interest that was due on the original thirty-year mortgage.

Table 4-5. Refinance Choices in the Market

	Original 30-year Fixed	Do Nothing	30-year Refinance	15-year Refinance
Principal	$150,000	$142,589	$142,589	$142,589
Interest rate	6.50%	6.50%	5.875%	5.500%
Monthly payment	$948.10	$948.10	$843.47	$1,165.07
Total interest to pay	$191,318.01	$191,318.01	$161,058.04	$67,123.88
Number of years of payments	4	30	30	15
Principal balance	$142,589.45	$0.00	$0.00	$0.00
Interest paid to date	$38,098.25	$191,318.01	$199,156.29	$105,222.13
Total savings			($7,838.28)	$86,095.88

Adding Costs, Fees, and Points to the Equation

So far we have not taken into consideration the additional costs associated with obtaining a mortgage, but they make a difference in both the short- and long-term financial impact of the refinancing. Attorney's fees, title search and insurance, appraisal fee, application fees, document preparation and filing fees, and brokerage fees and points can quickly add up to thousands of dollars. You can either pay them "out of pocket" at the closing, or add the costs into the amount of principal you are borrowing.

If you are paying the closing costs "out of pocket," one way to look at them, and to compare offers, is to calculate the length of time it will take you to recoup the costs from the monthly savings you get from the refinance. For example, if you save $200 per month on your mortgage payment and your closing costs are $6,000, it will take thirty months for you to recoup the costs. If you fund the costs of the mortgage by adding the amount to the principal, your monthly savings will be less, and your overall costs will increase because of the higher principal. (In Chapter 7 you will learn more about ways to compare financing offers, including costs.)

If you have substantial credit card debt or other significant loan obligations, the mortgage specialist who reviews your loan application and credit report should ask you whether you want to pay some or all of those obligations as part of the refinance transaction. If you are not certain, you should do the analysis for yourself, and ask the mortgage specialist to prepare a comparison for you, if he or she has not already done so.

Start with the "do nothing" option. What will your financial situation be if you do not refinance? Look at your current budget and try to predict how easily you will be able to shoulder your current and anticipated monthly bills.

Next, look at the options of refinancing the minimum amount of principal you can. In most cases that will be your present mortgage balance, unless you are unable to pay the estimated closing costs "out of pocket." If you do not have the cash to pay the costs, add them into the refinance principal; this is the minimum amount to borrow. Once you know what the monthly payment for the refinanced loan will be, use your budget as a tool to see what the impact will be on your cash flow. Do the calculations shown in Tables 4-1 and 4-2 to determine how much the new mortgage will cost you in total interest paid. Then decide whether it is worth it.

If you have debt that you would like to pay by taking cash out at the time you refinance, determine whether you can borrow enough to pay all that debt. Based on the LTV ratio of 80 percent, you can determine the maximum amount of principal a lender will make available to you. If this amount is more than enough to pay your debts, add your debt to the principal you need for your mortgage balance, and compute the monthly payment. Plug this new number into your budget and see how things look. Then, determine what the maximum amount is that you can borrow and still fall within the guidelines for limits on the housing ratio. Analyze the long-term impact as well.

If the maximum amount you could borrow is not enough to pay all your debt, look at your outstanding balances and the interest rate you are paying on the debt you are carrying with each creditor. Plan to pay off the highest-interest rate balances first. Assuming your refinanced mortgage is at the same or lower interest rate as your other obligations, you will be able to reduce your debt to income ratio by paying off the higher-interest debt.

This is well and good, assuming you do not get yourself back into debt. However, if you are counting on the equity in your home to continually bail you out of poor financial habits, a downturn in the economy or tightening lending guidelines could leave you unable to pay your bills or your mortgage, and unable to keep your home. Do not fall into this trap. If you are unable to pay all your debt with your refinancing options, use at least part of the monthly savings you realize to pay down the remaining debt. If you follow these guidelines, refinancing will put you in a better financial position immediately and for the future.

CHAPTER

KNOW YOUR CREDIT SCORE

A lender's decision to grant you a mortgage is based largely on the scores it uses to assess the likelihood you will repay the loan according to its terms, and if you fail to do that, the likelihood it will be able to sell your property at a price sufficient to recover the amount you owe. In Chapter 1 you learned that lenders look at three things when determining whether to lend you money, and if so, at what price: property value, income, and credit. LTV ratio is a score on property value relative to the loan amount. Housing ratio and debt to income ratio are income scores. Your credit score is the single biggest factor that determines how much you will pay for a mortgage.

If you don't know your scores, and if you don't understand the credit scoring guidelines for the most favorable loan terms, you don't know how attractive you look to a lender. And that means you could be a target for unscrupulous people to make a lot of money by selling you an unnecessarily expensive mortgage. To prevent that from happening, in this chapter you will learn:

☑ How to understand your credit report and credit score

☑ How to correct your credit report

☑ How to improve your credit score

Understanding Your Credit Report and Credit Score

Your credit report is one of the most significant pieces of information a lender uses to determine whether you qualify for a loan, and if so, how much of a premium you will pay above the best rates available. It tells a prospective lender how responsible you are and whether you pay your bills on time, and how well you manage the credit you have. Your credit score, which is one piece of information on your credit report, provides a concise picture of how you compare to other borrowers and the degree of risk a lender assumes by providing you with additional credit.

Three credit bureaus, Experian, Equifax, and TransUnion, provide your credit report to lenders, either directly or through credit agencies that combine information from these bureaus, and provide additional information or services for a fee. The data that goes into your credit report comes from credit transactions reported to the bureaus by the businesses and organizations that extend credit to you, such as stores, banks with which you have car loans, student loans or mortgages, and credit card companies.

Businesses and organizations request a credit report for almost any offer of credit, including store charges, gasoline cards, credit cards, and loans, and for purposes of employment, rental leases, and insurance. Again, it gives the reader a quick assessment of how you operate with regard to managing credit and paying your credit obligations.

Why should you know what your credit report tells lenders? One reason is to verify that the information contained in it is accurate. Another is that it can alert you to identity theft activities, where someone gets credit in your name, runs up the bills, and doesn't pay them, leaving you with a major credit problem.

The most important reason for you to know your score and what your credit report says is because you can improve that score over time, and that can make a big difference in how much you pay for a mortgage. Table 5-1 illustrates the effect of credit scores on the average interest rate for a thirty-year, fixed-rate mortgage of $150,000.

You can see that the difference in monthly payment and total interest due between an excellent credit score (760–850) and a poor one (620–639) is substantial. The monthly payment for a borrower with an excellent credit score is only $861 compared to $1,017 for the borrower with a poor score. The difference in interest rates means that the borrower with the poor credit score pays $216,178 interest, which is more than $56,000 higher than the $160,002 that the excellent-credit borrower will pay. You also can see that an increase in score of as little as thirty points, for example between 650 and 680, saves you money each month (monthly payments of $962 and $920 respec-

Table 5-1. Comparison of Interest Rates Based on Credit Scores
Thirty-year fixed-rate $150,000 mortgage

	Score Ranges					
	620–639	640–659	660–679	680–699	700–759	760–850
Interest rate	7.19%	6.64%	6.21%	6.00%	5.82%	5.60%
Monthly payment	$1,017	$962	$920	$899	$882	$861
Total interest due	$216,178	$196,307	$181,082	$173,755	$167,535	$160,002

tively) and thousands of dollars over the life of the loan ($196,307 compared to $181,082).

Requesting Your Credit Report

The Federal Trade Commission (FTC) enforces the Fair Credit Reporting Act, which governs how credit bureaus report your credit. By law, you have the right to receive a free copy of your credit report once per year from each credit bureau, but you must request it. You can order a copy of your report from each credit bureau at a single, shared website, www.annualcreditreport.com, or by phone or mail. The FTC warns that other websites with names similar to the official annualcreditreport.com site promise free credit reports but require that you purchase other services to receive it. You do not have to pay anything to receive your credit report at the official site. And neither the credit bureaus nor annualcreditreport.com will ever solicit your business or request personal information in a phone call or e-mail message. If you receive this type of solicitation, beware, and report the incident to the FTC at spam@uce.gov.

When you request your credit report, you will have to provide information that proves your identity, including your name, address, social security number, date of birth, and other information that only you would know, such as the amount of your mortgage payment. If you request your report online, you can access it immediately. Allow fifteen days for reports requested by phone or mail.

If you are denied employment, insurance, or credit, you are entitled to a free copy of your report if you request it within sixty days of the denial. If you are unemployed and plan to seek work within sixty days, or if you are on welfare, or if your report is inaccurate due to fraud or identity theft, you are entitled to another free report a year.

If you need additional copies of your report within a twelve-month period for reasons other than those stated, the credit bureau may charge you up to $10.50 per additional report.

Navigating the Mortgage Minefield: Establishing Credit If You Have No Credit History

If you have never borrowed money before, and if you do not have or use credit cards, you may not have a credit report or a credit score. College students, recent graduates, and newly divorced women are likely to fall into this category. In order for a credit bureau to give you a credit score, you must have a recently updated credit account that is at least six months old. You can still qualify for a loan without a credit report if you can show a paper trail of on-time payments for items such as rent and utilities. Your lender will specify the number and types of documents required to substitute for your credit report.

Not all creditors report information to credit bureaus; for example, gasoline card companies and local retailers do not normally report transactions to the credit bureaus. If you have a history of good credit with these nonreporting businesses, you can request, for a fee, that the credit bureau add this information, one-time, to your credit report. Updates to the information will not be available unless you request it and pay for it again.

To establish credit, you can open a bank account if you do not already have one, and apply for a credit card that you can manage from a business that reports transactions to credit bureaus. You can start with a department store charge card, which is easier to get than a Visa or Master Card. Once you have established a consistent record of on-time payments over several months, you can apply for a Visa, Master Card or similar credit card. This will help build your credit.

Above all else, pay your bills on time. Late payments hurt your credit score, no matter what your reason for them. Manage your credit responsibly by paying your balance in full each month to avoid finance charges and accumulating debt.

What Determines Your Credit Score

Each credit bureau has its own method for determining your credit score, based on the information they have about your use of available credit and your credit history. Credit agencies combine your credit reports from the three credit bureaus to provide lenders with a complete picture of your credit. A lender will usually look at the middle score or average the scores when deciding how much to charge you for the money you want to borrow.

The Fair Isaac Corporation developed a method for calculating scores, referred to as the FICO score, which is a widely used standard. Scores range from 300 to 850. The higher the score, the more creditworthy lenders consider you to be. Lenders group credit scores into categories or grades ranging from excellent to poor. The number of categories or grades, and the range of scores that fall into each one, vary by lender, and fluctuate with general credit market conditions; at one point, scores of 720 were in the highest category, but now you need a score of 750 or better to qualify for the best rates.

When you apply for a mortgage, the loan originator will ask you about your outstanding credit balances, and whether you have any recent late payments. It is important that you know this information and that you are truthful with the originator. When the originator gets your official credit report, one of the things he or she will look at is how honest and knowledgeable you are about your finances. This tells the originator how responsible you are, and even if your credit is less than perfect, your responsible attitude is important.

What Goes into Your FICO Score. Your FICO score is based on five types of information that are weighted and used in a formula that was derived from statistical analysis of many thousands of borrowers. Your payment history counts for 35 percent of your score, which is why late payments are so damaging. Recent late payments will hurt you more than older ones, so time can help improve your score in this area.

The second type of information, which accounts for about 30 percent of your score, involves how much you owe, the number of accounts to whom you owe it, and the percentage of your available credit you are using. The higher the percentage of your credit limits you carry in open balances, the lower your score. Carrying balances that are more than 50 percent of your credit limit hurts your score.

The third category of information used to compute your credit score is the age of your credit history, and it accounts for about 15 percent of your score. Keep old credit accounts open, even if they are inactive, to maximize points in this category.

The fourth type of information, accounting for 10 percent of your FICO score, involves new credit, including any inquiries regarding your credit by perspective lenders, regardless of whether they grant you a loan. The scoring is sophisticated enough to distinguish patterns of multiple inquiries for a single credit account from inquiries for multiple accounts. If you apply for several credit cards in a short period, it hurts your score. Shopping for a mortgage will not, if you do it within a short period.

The final category of information used to calculate your credit score, accounting for about 10 percent of your score, is a catch-all for other factors such as having a mix of credit types, such as credit card, auto loan, mortgage, and lines of credit, which helps your score.

Race, color, religion, national origin, gender, marital status, and whether you receive public assistance are all factors that cannot be used to determine your credit score, according to federal law.

Navigating the Mortgage Minefield: Other Factors That Compensate for Poor Scores

If your credit score is not great, or if your LTV, debt to income, or housing ratios are not perfect, you still may be able to qualify for a loan at a good rate. Lenders, including Fannie Mae and Freddie Mac, use other information about your finances to compensate for low scores in one area. Three favorable compensating factors can balance one less-than-ideal score, so even with a mediocre credit score it is still possible to qualify for a good loan.

One of the compensating factors that a lender considers to offset a less-than-ideal ratio or credit score is your *reserves*, the financial assets you have in savings accounts, retirement accounts, pension funds, money market accounts, and investments. The lender discounts the amount you have in retirement plans, such as a 401(k), if you are not fully vested. Reserves assure the lender that if you fall on rough financial times you have enough money to continue making your mortgage payments for a period until you get back on financial track. Reserves sufficient to cover more than three months of housing expense can compensate for higher housing ratios or debt to income ratios than standard for conforming loans.

Long-term steady employment at the same job can also compensate for less than ideal credit scores, LTV, or income ratios. A history of employment at the same job indicates stability and reliability, and predicts continued employment in the future.

Finally, an excellent credit score, combined with other favorable compensating factors such as substantial reserves and steady employment at the same company have resulted in approval for conforming loans with very high debt to income ratios that might result from a relatively large mortgage. Taken together the compensating factors show an ongoing pattern of responsible financial behavior that offsets the lender's risk.

How to Read Your Credit Report

Regardless of the reporting credit bureau or agency, your credit report will contain sections for identification and residence information, public records, credit inquiries, credit score, and credit history, each of which is explained in the sections that follow.

Identification and Residence Information. The identification section of the credit report contains information to uniquely identify you. The report shows your name, social security number, date of birth, address, and how long you have lived there.

Public Records. The public records section of the report contains information about bankruptcies, lawsuits, judgments, foreclosures, and other matters of public record affecting your credit. It details the date, description, and status of each matter.

Credit Inquiries. Every time a potential creditor requests your credit report, the event is recorded. More than three inquiries in a two-week period can drop your score by thirty-five points or more, which could have a big impact on how much you pay for your loan. Why are excessive inquiries detrimental? They indicate that you are seeking credit, which, if you are already overextended, can indicate a potential credit problem. Don't apply for credit unless you need it, and if you do, shop around before you fill out the application or authorize a creditor to access your credit report.

Credit Score. In addition to reporting your score, the credit report includes an explanation of items that negatively affected the score. Common reasons cited for deductions to credit scores are "Proportion of balances to credit limits is too high on bank revolving or other revolving accounts," "Number of accounts with delinquency," "Too many inquiries last 12 months," and "Length of time accounts have been established."

Credit History. The credit history section of your report lists each credit account, and for each one, the creditor, the age of the account, your credit limit, the type of account, the account number, the minimum monthly payment, and a history, by month, for the last two years, of whether your payments were received on time. Any creditor with whom you have done business in the last ten years, even if your account is closed, may be reported in this section. The longer an account has been open, even if not active, the better for your score.

Car loans, student loans, credit cards, store charge cards, and your current mortgage, if you have one, all appear in this section. A string of numbers, one for each month, depict your payment history, with "1" meaning your payment was on time for the month, and "2" meaning your payment was late. A tally of late payments by length of delinquency shows for each account and payments that are more than thirty-days overdue are most damaging to your score. Mortgage lenders place less emphasis on late payments for credit cards or store charge accounts than they do on late payments for auto, student, and mortgage loans or rent. Late payments on these types of accounts are most damaging to your credit report. They are "red flags" to lenders that give the impression that either you are not responsible in handling your financial obligations or you are unable to meet them. The more recent the late payment, the more detrimental it will be to your score. Payments that are sixty-days late or more could prevent you from getting a loan you can afford.

Correcting Your Credit Report

Credit reporting is not 100 percent accurate, and credit bureaus are fallible. If you believe there is information in your credit report that is not accurate, and that it is hurting your credit score, take steps to have the mistake corrected. Do not assume that the mistake will correct itself—it won't. And don't delay: The process can take up to six weeks, and during that time your credit is affected. The correction process does not cost anything, and you can find specific details for filing a dispute for each of the three credit bureaus at their websites:

☑ www.equifax.com/online-credit-dispute

☑ www.transunion.com/corporate/personal/creditDisputes.page

☑ www.experian.com/disputes2/index.html

In all cases, have your report in front of you for reference when you file the dispute. While all three credit bureaus encourage online filing of disputes, the Federal Citizen Information Center, an office of the U.S. General Services Administration, recommends you file by certified, return receipt mail, and include copies (not originals) of all relevant documents that support your claim. For more information and a sample dispute letter, go to www.pueblo.gsa.gov/coc_text/money/credit-record/crrecord.htm.

Once you file a dispute, either by phone, by mail, or online, the credit bureau initiates an investigation with the party who provided the information, usually a creditor, a collection agency, or a court. You should receive a response within thirty to forty-five days. If the information you are disputing is, in fact, inaccurate, the credit bureau corrects it. If the information is accurate, but nonetheless unfavorable, it remains on your credit report. Beware of companies that claim to be able to remove unfavorable but accurate information from your report—they cannot do it and they are ripping you off. Unfavorable but accurate information can remain on your credit report for seven years, and bankruptcy information can remain for ten years.

If you are applying for a loan and the disputed item is lowering your credit score, notify your prospective lender that you are disputing the item. If you document the error and the fact that you initiated the correction process, a lender may consider the correction when deciding on your loan. If not, you will have to wait until your lender can obtain a corrected report and updated credit score to get a better rate on your loan. If you request it, the credit bureau is required to send a corrected credit report to anyone who requested a report within six months, and to do so at no charge to you.

How to Improve Your Credit Score

Your credit score reflects the way you operate with regard to money. If your score is hurting your ability to obtain affordable credit, you can change the way you operate, and if you do, can improve your score with time.

Create a budget. Stick to it. Begin operating with integrity around your finances immediately and consistently. Get into the habit of paying your bills on time. Start paying off credit card balances so your balances are no more than 50 percent of your credit limits. If you reduce your debt, your debt to income ratio will improve. Remember, lenders give the best rates to people who have debt to income ratios of 36 percent or less. Pay small, recently reported accounts first, so you have fewer open accounts and the changes have a positive effect sooner. Keep receipts for all your payments, because it may take some time for updated balances to appear on your credit report, and sometimes lenders accept receipts as proof of payment.

If you are unable to pay your bills, call your creditors before they turn your account over to a collection agency. Offer to work out a payment plan with them, and avoid the heavy negative effect that a collection action has on your credit score.

If your credit score reflects too many inquiries, you can raise it and save thousands of dollars by waiting thirty days to apply for a mortgage. During that waiting period, do not apply for any credit, and by the end of that period your excessive inquiries will have expired and will no longer bring your score down.

Only you can take steps necessary to improve your credit score. It starts with a commitment on your part to change the way you operate, and it requires that you take appropriate actions consistently over time. You can do it!

RECOGNIZE WHICH LOAN PRODUCT IS RIGHT FOR YOU

Fixed or adjustable? Thirty-year or fifteen? Points, rates, closing costs? There are many loan options from which to choose, and it can seem overwhelming unless you know what is important to you and what you are trying to achieve financially. Unless your credit is horrible, there is likely to be a lender who, for a high enough price, will lend you money. You are responsible for making sure you understand the terms and can afford the loan.

In this chapter you will learn:

- ☑ How to decide whether a fixed-rate or adjustable-rate mortgage is best for you

- ☑ What your repayment options are and what effect they have on monthly payments and overall cost

- ☑ What qualifications are required for special types of mortgages

- ☑ What special mortgage features are available and how much they cost

Fixed-Rate or Adjustable-Rate: Which Is Better for You?

In spite of many variations, basically there are only two classes of mortgages: fixed-rate or adjustable-rate. To recap, a fixed-rate mortgage has the same rate of interest and monthly payment for the entire term of the loan. An adjustable-rate mortgage's interest rate changes periodically at preset intervals over the term of the loan, changing the monthly payment amount. A *hybrid* mortgage is a variation of an adjustable-rate mortgage that has an initial fixed-rate period of several years, after which the rate adjusts periodically.

Your credit, income, and LTV, housing, and debt to income ratios largely determine the lowest interest rate available to you, but you can trade off term and points to lower your monthly payment. There also are several features of which you can take advantage that will alter your interest rate and monthly payment.

How Long Will You Keep the Mortgage?

One question to ask when deciding whether a fixed-rate or adjustable-rate mortgage is better for you is "How long do I expect to live in this house?" That may seem like an odd question, but it makes sense when you realize that hybrid mortgages, which are technically adjustable-rate mortgages, can provide you the advantages of both a fixed-rate and adjustable-rate mortgage, as long as you sell your home within the initial fixed-rate period. A hybrid usually has a lower interest rate during the initial fixed-rate period than a comparable fixed-rate mortgage. As long as you sell your home and pay off the mortgage before the initial fixed-rate period ends, you have the security of a fixed-rate mortgage at the lower price of an adjustable-rate mortgage.

Table 6-1 compares the rates and payments for a 7/1 ARM, a fifteen-year fixed-rate, and a thirty-year fixed-rate. You can see that the interest rate on the ARM is lower than the fifteen-year, as is the monthly payment, whereas the fifteen-year rate is lower than the thirty-year, but the monthly payment is higher. The reason is that the ARM amortizes the principal over thirty years, so you get the double benefit with the hybrid of the lower rates and lower payments. If you plan to be in your home for less than seven years, or know you will refinance within seven years, a fixed-rate and an adjustable-rate hybrid are both good options.

If you consider a hybrid as a short-term loan, you must be certain that the initial fixed-rate period is longer than the time you will stay in your home. A miscalculation could leave you in a very bad financial position. The interest rate on that ARM could jump as much as five percentage points to 10.125 at the end of seven years, and you would be facing a monthly payment of over $1,400.

Are You Averse to Risk?

Another question to ask when deciding between a fixed-rate or adjustable-rate mortgage is "How comfortable am I with the risk that my monthly mortgage payment could go up?" For some people, the answer is a quick and unequivocal "Not comfortable at all!" They simply want to know what the payment will be and want to know that

Table 6-1. Comparison of 7/1 ARM with 15- and 30-Year Fixed Rate

	7/1 ARM	15-Year	30-Year
Principal	$150,000	$150,000	$150,000
Interest rate	5.125%	5.250%	5.750%
Monthly payment	$817	$1,206	$875

it will stay that way. If you are one of those people, stick with a fixed-rate mortgage product.

If you can comfortably handle the risk that your mortgage payment will increase, consider the worst case scenario. How much of an increase could you bear without hardship? This question is difficult to answer objectively unless you have a budget and know your monthly income and expenses. If you don't have much discretionary income at the end of each month, don't bet your home that interest rates will drop or your income will rise. If, however, you have a substantial surplus each month and an increase of one or two percentage points won't alter your lifestyle, and if you don't mind that your monthly payment will change, then stay open to the possibility of an adjustable-rate mortgage.

Payment Choices

Over the term of the loan, or when you sell or refinance, you will pay back the principal you borrowed and the interest charged for using the money. Remember that the longer you use the money, the more interest you pay. Regardless of whether you choose a fixed-rate or adjustable-rate mortgage, you have several repayments options, many related to the timing of interest and principal payment, that each affects how much money you repay in total.

Should You Pay Points?

Points are a percentage of the loan amount that you pay at the closing. Points are, in effect, a prepayment of interest on the loan. *Par* is the term used for the interest rate at which you pay zero points. You can increase points to "buy down" or discount the interest rate on the loan, thereby reducing the monthly payments. The more points you pay up front at the closing, the larger the discount on the interest rate, and the lower your monthly payment.

Is it a smart decision to pay points to reduce your monthly payment? It depends, once again, on how long you hold the mortgage before you sell the house or refinance. If the best par rate you can get for a $150,000 thirty-year fixed-rate loan is 5.75 percent, and you pay one discount point ($1,500), you may get a discount of up to 0.250 percent, or a rate of 5.5 percent. Your monthly payment will be $852, a monthly savings of about $23.

To calculate the number of months you have to keep the mortgage to recoup your discount points, divide the dollar amount of the points by your monthly payment savings. Divide that number by twelve to know how many years of monthly savings it takes for you to break even with the cost of the points. If you don't keep your mortgage at least that long, you paid more in points than they were worth in savings.

Continuing the example above, you pay $1,500 at the closing to save $23 per month for up to thirty years. Dividing $1,500 by $23 per month gives a break-even point of sixty-five months, or almost five and a half years ($65/12 = 5$ years $+ 5$ months). If you keep your home and do not refinance within five and a half years, it makes sense for you to pay the points. If, on the other hand, you are not sure, or you know that you may sell or refinance within that time, consider what else you could do with that $1,500. Could you use it for household expenses or improvements and avoid higher-interest credit card debt? Or could you afford to invest it and earn some interest?

Flexible Monthly Payment Options: Short- and Long-Term Benefits and Risks

Traditional fixed-rate mortgages offer one way of paying: A portion of every monthly payment is applied to principal and a portion of each payment is applied to interest. The allocation of the monthly payment between principal and interest changes with each payment, with most of the early payments heavily applied to interest. The total dollar amount remains the same over the term of the loan.

A portion of your monthly payment for an adjustable-rate mortgage reduces your principal owed, but because the interest varies over the term of the loan, your payment amount fluctuates with changes in the interest rate. In most cases, unless otherwise specified, your monthly payment includes all the interest that is due for that month, plus some portion of the principal.

An *interest-only mortgage (I-O)* is one for which payments during an initial fixed-period consist only of interest, and you start paying the principal at the end of the initial fixed period. Most I-Os have initial-fixed periods of three to ten years. After the initial fixed period, they either adjust annually, or can convert to a fixed-rate.

Some mortgages, both fixed-rate and adjustable-rate, allow you to choose the type of payment you make in any particular month. You can pay the standard payment, which includes interest and principal, or you may choose an interest-only payment or a minimum payment, which is less than the interest-only payment. Flexible payment mortgages are great for people who have income that fluctuates throughout the year, because it allows them to reduce their monthly payment in months where money is tight, and potentially make it up in months when they are flush.

When you make minimum or interest-only payments, you do not build the equity in your home or reduce the balance you owe, even though you make a payment. In fact, when you make a minimum payment, you increase the amount you owe, because the payment is not sufficient to cover the interest due, and the unpaid interest adds to the amount you owe (and the amount on which you pay interest in the future).

ARMs with payment options have very low introductory rates, in the range of 1 to 2 percent, for a few months, but then rates tend to rise to levels closer to standard ARMs. Your minimum payment amount is based on the introductory rate, and there is usually a cap on how much the minimum payment can increase in any one adjustment period. For example, if the cap on the minimum payment is 5 percent, your minimum payment will not increase by more than 5 percent, even if interest rates increase by more than that amount. If you continue to make minimum payments, you continue to increase the amount of money you owe, even though you pay money every month.

At preset intervals or when the principal reaches a certain limit—for example, 125 percent of the original loan—the lender *recasts* the mortgage. Recasting amortizes the principal balance due over the remaining term of the loan. If you've been making minimum payments for several years and your principal balance is now greater than the original loan amount, the lender will recast the larger balance over the term that remains on the original loan. When that happens, your monthly payment could double or triple, shocking you unless you understand the terms of the loan and the risks associated with option payments.

In addition to the risk of shocking increases in monthly payments and negative amortization, there are other potential dangers with interest-only and minimum-payment options. You may not be able to refinance before the adjustments or recasts increase your monthly payment; prevailing interest rates could make refinancing unfeasible, or if real estate values drop you could owe more than the house is worth and not be able to refinance or sell your home for enough to cover your debt. And option-payment ARMs and I-Os, as well as other mortgages, can charge you money for paying off your mortgage earlier than the term in which it is due. Prepayment penalties can run into thousands of dollars, affecting the cost of refinancing.

When Are I-Os and Option Payment Mortgages Good Choices?

Under the right conditions, an interest-only or option-payment mortgage is a good choice that can save you money and help your cash flow. If you know for certain that your income is going to increase substantially—if, for example, if you are completing education that qualifies you for a raise at your job—then these payment options can allow you to "grow into" a more expensive home. If your income does not come evenly throughout the year because of periodic bonuses, commissions, or seasonal fluctuations, these payment options allow you to adjust your payments to your flow of income. Remember, though, when the income does come in, to make this arrangement work you have to put more money toward your mortgage, not spend it elsewhere.

If you have a large amount of equity in your home, and you can invest the money that would go toward principal at a higher interest rate than you are paying on the mortgage, an interest-only ARM allows you to do that. Keep careful watch on interest rates, the housing market, and the return on your investment to ensure that interest-only payments continue to be the best use of your money.

Navigating the Mortgage Minefield: Focusing Only on the Monthly Payment Can Get You into a House You Cannot Afford

Low introductory interest rates for payment-option and interest-only mortgages can get you into real trouble when you purchase a home by qualifying you to purchase a house you cannot really afford. If you focus only on the monthly payment, without paying close attention to the full terms of the mortgage behind it, you make a big mistake. That kind of thinking can lead you to decisions that put you at risk of losing your home.

If your budget allows for a monthly mortgage payment of $1,100, at today's rates you could get a conventional thirty-year fixed-rate mortgage of about $180,000. You will pay $1,100 a month, never more, for thirty years, or until you sell or refinance.

The same $1,100 per month payment could get you more principal, say $215,000, with an interest-only or option-payment mortgage. If you buy a more expensive home, you will be in big trouble when the rates adjust or the interest-only period ends. And if you had been making minimum payments rather than interest-only payments, at the time of the adjustment you could owe more than your home is worth, making it impossible to refinance.

Use your budget to know the maximum monthly payment you can afford. If you take advantage of an option-payment or interest-only mortgage that results in a lower monthly payment for some period, know the caps on your mortgage and make sure that if the worst happens and your rate increases to the cap at the earliest possible time, the resulting monthly payment is still within your budget.

Accelerated Payments

Mortgage payments are due monthly, twelve times per year. With an accelerated payment plan, you pay half the monthly payment amount every other week. These biweekly payments, twenty-six per year, have the effect of making thirteen monthly payments, which is one extra monthly payment per year. Most people, especially if they are paid biweekly, do not notice the difference in their cash flow, but the savings on the mortgage is substantial. By making the equivalent of one extra monthly payment per year, you can pay off a thirty-year fixed-rate mortgage in about twenty-three years, saving you thousands of dollars in interest and building your equity more quickly.

Banks and other lenders that offer and may charge for accelerated payment plans accept the "extra payment" as a combination of interest and principal. You can boost the savings and the speed with which you build equity if you manage the biweekly payment plan yourself and have the extra payment applied in full to reducing the principal balance. Put aside some money for the extra payment with every paycheck until you have accumulated enough for a payment, and then send it to your lender with a letter indicating you want the payment applied to principal.

Balloon Payments and Two-Step Mortgages

Some fixed-rate and adjustable-rate mortgages, particularly those designed to be paid back in a short period, are not fully amortized, which means that at the end of the loan term you must pay the principal balance in a lump sum called the *balloon payment*. With this type of mortgage, your monthly payment is based on a thirty-year amortization, which has very low principal payments in the early years. If the note is due in seven years rather than thirty, you have to pay the principal balance at that time. If you have substantial equity in your home and know you will be selling before the balloon payment is due, this option is one you should consider. As with the hybrids, however, if you miscalculate the timing of the sale you may not be able to come up with the cash, and if that happens, you could lose your home.

To minimize the risk associated with the balloon payment, some lenders offer a *two-step* or *reset* option with balloon payment mortgages. When the balloon payment is due, the note "resets" at prevailing fixed rates and fully amortizes. The lender may specify conditions you must meet to reset the mortgage, including requirements that you continue to reside in the home, that there are no other liens on the property, and that you have made all mortgage payments on time.

A two-step mortgage can be an effective way for you to get a home if your credit is not great and you take the steps necessary to improve it during the period prior to the reset. If you use the savings from the lower monthly payment to pay off debt and improve your scores and ratios, you can qualify for better rates when the note resets than you may be eligible for now. Beware that if you don't do what is necessary to improve your position, you may be ineligible for the reset and may have to sell your home to pay the balloon.

Special Mortgages for Those Who Qualify

The U.S. government encourages home ownership through a number of lending programs, each of which has its own specific eligibility requirements. The FHA, which is part of HUD, does not lend money directly, but insures mortgages with approved lenders under programs for first-time home buyers, the elderly, and renovations. The Veteran's Administration provides loans to qualified individuals who served in the military. Visit www.hud.gov/buying/loans.cfm or www .homeloans.va.gov for detailed and current information about these programs and their eligibility requirements.

FHA Loans

The FHA boasts several advantages to obtaining FHA-insured loans through approved lenders. You benefit from lower rates and less stringent qualifying requirements because FHA insures the loan repayment, minimizing the lender's risk if you default. This means it will be easier for you to qualify for a mortgage, especially if your credit is not good or you have gone through bankruptcy. Down payments on FHA loans can be as low as 3 percent, and don't restrict the source of the funds. That means you can borrow the down payment from your family or employer.

First-Time Home Buyer's Program. Even if you have owned a home in the past, there are certain conditions under which you still qualify for an FHA loan as a first-time home buyer: If you are buying a home you will live in and have not owned a home in three years; if you are divorced and are a displaced homemaker or single parent, you may qualify even if you owned a home with your former spouse; if you are buying a home you will live in with someone who qualifies as a first-time home buyer.

Good Neighbor Next Door Program. If you are a teacher, police officer, firefighter, or emergency medical technician, HUD's Good Neighbor Next Door program can grant you a 50 percent discount on the purchase price of qualified homes in HUD-designated revitalization areas in exchange for your guarantee to occupy the property for three years. HUD requires that you sign a second mortgage for the discount amount, but no payments are required if you fulfill the three-year residency requirement.

Renovation Loans. Part of HUD's mission is to increase home ownership in low-income communities, and it provides incentives for people who are willing to rehabilitate, renovate, and restore run-down properties in these neighborhoods. Since the market value of a home in need of rehabilitation is not always sufficient to support a mortgage large enough to include the renovation costs, HUD provides insurance to lenders so they lend based on the projected value of the home as if it were already renovated. There are requirements and restrictions on the types of homes and renovations that are eligible for this funding, so check with HUD and your lender, or go to www.hud.gov/offices/hsg/sfh/203k/203kabou.cfm for details.

Reverse Mortgages for the Elderly. If you are sixty-two years of age or older, and you have significant equity in your home, you may qualify for a HUD-insured reverse mortgage. A reverse mortgage provides cash flow benefits and security. It pays you each month from the equity in your home, but unlike a home equity loan, you do not have to repay any interest or principal until you no longer use the home as your primary residence. You cannot default on the loan since there is nothing to pay, and HUD insures that you do not have to pay back more than your house is worth when you sell it, regardless of how much you have borrowed.

You have several options for receiving payments with a reverse mortgage. Like a fixed-rate mortgage, *tenure payments* remain fixed in amount for the life of the loan. *Term payments* are also fixed, but for a predetermined length of time. *Line of credit payments* work like a HELOC: You take payments, as you need them, at any time. You can combine line of credit payment options with either tenure payments or term payments, These options, referred to as *modified tenure* and *modified term*, respectively, give you maximum flexibility and control.

Learn more about HUD-insured reverse mortgages at www.hud .gov/offices/hsg/sfh/hecm/rmtopten.cfm.

Veteran's Administration Loans

If you are a veteran of the U.S. armed services and meet requirements for length of duty and discharge, you may be eligible for a *Veteran's Administration (VA) loan*. As with FHA loans, VA loans have less stringent requirements for credit and income qualification and LTV than conventional mortgages. No-down-payment loans are possible, and you can finance PMI, closing costs, and VA-required fees. Rates are competitive or lower than conventional mortgages, but not determined by the VA; as with the FHA, the VA does not lend directly, but deals through approved lenders who may have their own restrictions and policies.

You will have to provide a Certificate of Eligibility to the lender. Instructions for obtaining this certificate are at www.homeloans.va .gov/eligibility.htm. You also must use the home, which must be located in the United States or its territories or possessions, as your primary residence to be eligible.

Special Features of Mortgages and What They Cost

The interest rate on a mortgage can go up because of features that you wish to take advantage of in the loan process itself, in the terms of the loan, or in the manner in which you make payments monthly. Points are added to the par interest rate for anything that increases the lender's risk, including locking the interest rate between approval and closing, limited or no income documentation, high LTV, principal amounts larger than conforming loan limits, and waiver of escrow for real estate taxes. Each of these features has a benefit to certain borrowers, but they each come with a cost.

Rate Locks

The time between approval of a mortgage by a lender and the mortgage closing, particularly with a home purchase, can often be several months. During that time, the prevailing interest rates for both fixed- and adjustable-rate loans fluctuate. If you want the lender to guarantee that the rate for which you were approved is the rate you will get at the closing (and thus the monthly payment you expect will not change), the lender will charge you extra, in the form of a slightly higher interest rate. The longer the period for which you want the guarantee, the higher the premium will be. These guarantees, or *rate locks*, are advantageous to you as a borrower when interest rates are rising; as long as you close on your loan within the designated lock period, the lender cannot raise the interest rate on your loan. Rate locks can work against you when rates are falling, and prevent you from taking advantage of lower rates that become available. Rate lock periods range from seven days to several months, and add or subtract from an eighth of a point (0.125) to over two points to your interest rate. These locks have expiration dates, and if you need to extend your lock or it expires, it will either cost you more to reinstate it, or subject you to a change in rate.

Some lenders give you the best of both worlds: A *float down* protects you against rising rates, but lets you take advantage of a drop in rates. Of course, it costs extra, too, but if your closing is weeks away and your expected payment is close to the limit of what you can afford, it may be worth it to protect your budget and have peace of mind until your loan closes.

Jumbo Mortgages

Fannie Mae and Freddie Mac, the government-backed enterprises that buy conventional mortgages from lenders, set limits on the amount of principal for conforming loans. Table 6-2 shows conforming loan maximum amounts that went into effect on January 1, 2008. Current maximums are posted at www.fanniemae.com/aboutfm/loanlimits.jhtml.

If you need to borrow more than the maximum, your lender will tack a premium onto the interest rate to compensate for greater difficulty selling the loan in the secondary market. Premiums on a thirty-

Table 6-2. Maximum Conforming Loan Amounts
(Effective January 1, 2008)

	Single-Family	Two-Family	Three-Family	Four-Family	Second Mortgage
48 Contiguous States	$417,000	$533,850	$645,300	$801,950	$208,500
Alaska, Hawaii, Guam, US Virgin Is.	$625,500	$800,775	$967,950	$1,202,925	$312,750

year fixed-rate mortgage range from 1/2 percent (0.50 percent) to 2 percent.

Loans for New Construction

If you are building a home, or buying a home that is not yet fully constructed, you can apply for a loan to cover the cost of construction. Typically, construction loans require interest-only payments until the construction is complete and you obtain a certificate of occupancy. A *certificate of occupancy* is a document issued by an authorized inspector that states the building meets code standards and is fit to be lived in. The principal on a construction loan usually is due when the certificate of occupancy is issued. At that time you would seek a regular mortgage from which you would pay off the construction loan.

As with a traditional mortgage, the lender wants you to have a financial stake in repaying the loan, and will be looking at your equity in the property. If you own the land on which you are building, the value of the land is part of your equity. If not, then you may not be able to get 100 percent financing for the construction costs, and if you have less than 20 percent equity, your loan is subject to PMI. Construction loans are usually adjustable-rate, and short-term. You can set up the loan so that funds become available to you on a schedule or as each phase of the construction is completed, and you pay interest only on the funds that you have taken to date.

An alternative to a construction loan followed by a mortgage is a *construction-to-permanent financing*, which is a type of mortgage that converts a construction loan to a mortgage automatically when you receive the certificate of occupancy. The advantage is that you only have to apply for one loan, and there is only one closing, so the costs are lower than applying for and closing on two separate loans. Typically, the loan limit for construction-to-permanent financing is the cost of the land plus construction costs only, so if you are looking for additional cash through the financing, it may not be available to you with this loan product.

When you get a construction-to-permanent loan, the interest rate for the interest-only construction loan is set when you sign the agreement, but the rate for the permanent mortgage financing is set when the house is complete. Depending on the mortgage markets and the time between the start of construction and certificate of occupancy, rates could change dramatically. You can pay for a rate lock for the mortgage at the time you get the construction-to-permanent loan, but be sure that the expiration date is far enough into the future to cover your worst-case scenario if completion of your construction is delayed.

No Escrow Loans

Typically, a lender adds property taxes and insurance premiums to your monthly principal and interest payment and puts these funds into an escrow account until your tax or insurance bills are due. Requiring you to escrow these funds with them lets the lender know that the bills will be paid on time and in full, protecting their security interest in your home. You do not have to agree to the escrow, but it will cost you a quarter percent extra (0.250). If your income fluctuates, this option allows you to save for taxes and insurance when you have the money and helps cash flow. If you do not exercise discipline about saving the extra income when it comes in, allow the lender to escrow and adjust your budget or mortgage size accordingly.

Income, Asset, and Employment Documentation

Your loan application asks for information about your income, your assets such as savings and retirement accounts, and your employment. The information you provide tells the lender whether you have steady employment, make sufficient income to meet your housing and other debt commitments, and how much money you have in reserve should you temporarily lose your source of income. Lenders vary in the amount and type of documentation they require with the loan package. And any lender may offer mortgages with different levels and types of documentation and verification of the information provided.

In general, there are four levels of documentation: full documentation, limited documentation, stated, and none. There also are three levels of verification conducted by the lender: full verification of source and amount, verification of source but not amount, and no verification. Lenders offer combinations of documentation and verification levels. The least risky to the lender is full documentation, full verification; the most risky is no documentation (and with it, no verification). Other combinations fall in between these degrees of risk. To compensate for the added risk of anything riskier than full documentation, a lender charges a premium and may require lower LTV and higher credit scores. Full documentation, limited documentation, stated income, and no documentation loans are the most common, but each lender offers its own variations.

Full Documentation Loan. With a *full documentation loan*, you provide information about the source and amount of your income, the type and amounts of your assets, and details about your last two years of employment. To qualify for this type of loan you must be able to prove that you have been at your job or in your current business for at least two years. The lender verifies your income by requesting a copy of your tax return from the Internal Revenue Service, verifies your assets by requesting information from the institutions where your assets reside, and verifies your employment through written communication with your employer. A "full doc" loan is the least risky for a lender and the least expensive for you.

Limited Documentation Loan. A *limited documentation loan* requires the same level of documentation as the full documentation loan, and the same two-year income rule applies. The difference between the full documentation and "limited doc" loans is that with a limited documentation loan the lender accepts your W-2 as verification of income, your bank statements as verification of assets, and accepts a verbal verification of employment from your employer. Although a lender may not charge you a premium for a limited documentation loan, you may need a higher credit score to qualify for a limited doc loan than you do for a full doc.

Stated Income Loan. With a *stated income loan*, you disclose the amount of your income, and the lender verifies the source but not the amount. To qualify, you may have to document more assets, which the lender fully verifies. The lender accepts verbal verification of your employment. This arrangement is called *SIVA*, which stands for Stated Income, Verified Assets.

Stated-income loans are popular with self-employed borrowers and others who may not have steady income, such as those who work on commissions. Small-business owners and self-employed people are able to take advantage of certain tax deductions that reduce the amount of taxable income they show on tax returns, which makes their housing and debt to income ratios appear less favorable than if they earned the same amount from a fully taxable salary.

Stated income loans cost an additional 1/2 to 1 percent above full and limited documentation loans.

No Documentation Loans. If you cannot or do not wish to provide any information about your income, assets, or employment, you can apply for a *no documentation loan*, provided you have high credit scores. This is the riskiest scenario for a lender, and it commands a hefty premium.

CHAPTER 7

KNOW YOUR BOUNDARIES

S hopping for a mortgage is not very different from shopping for any product with variations and features; if you don't know exactly what you need and what you want, you are likely to buy the model that the most convincing salesperson sells you. It is easy to be persuaded, particularly when it is hard to directly compare one offer with another. This is why it is important to know what you want to accomplish with a mortgage. You want to be able to compare each offer you receive to a single standard—your requirements—and not waste time trying to compare them to one another.

In this chapter you will learn:

☑ How to develop several options that define parameters for a loan that meets your financial goals

☑ How calculating annual percentage rate helps you compare offers

Defining What You Need

Let's review the basics. What is your current financial situation and what happens if you do nothing? Table 7-1 is a worksheet you can use

Table 7-1. Loan Comparison Worksheet

		Current Situation	What I want/ need	Loan Option A	Loan Option B
My Requirements					
1	**My Monthly Income**				
	Housing Expense				
2	Monthly mortgage/ Rent payment				
3	Taxes				
4	Hazard insurance				
5	PMI				
6	PMI expiration at $				
7	**Total Housing Expense (Total Lines 2 through 5)**				
8	**Housing Ratio (Line 7 / Line 1)**				

to compare your current situation (the "do nothing" option), your goals, and different loan scenarios. (See Appendix A for complete form.)

The top section of the form focuses on your monthly income, housing, and debt expenses. When you complete your mortgage application, this is the information you supply to a lender. In addition to the structure it provides to compare loan options, this worksheet creates an opportunity for you to organize your records and prepare the information you'll need for the application.

Assessing Your Current Financial Situation

Your first step is to assess your current financial situation. Begin by computing your gross monthly income. If you receive a paycheck regularly, compute your monthly income by multiplying the gross wages on your pay stub by the number of times you get paid a year, and dividing by 12. For example, if your gross wages are $1,000 and you are paid weekly, your monthly gross income is ($1,000 × 52) divided by 12, or $4,333. If your wages fluctuate because of overtime, commissions, tips, or bonuses, estimate your average monthly income over the past two years.

Next, list all your debt obligations, entering the balance owed and the minimum monthly payment for each. When you start comparing different options, you will be able to see what happens to your monthly expenses if you use the mortgage to pay off some or all of your debt.

If you already have a mortgage and are planning to refinance or sell your home to buy another, complete the section of the worksheet beginning with line 20. Enter the estimated market value of your

Table 7-1. Loan Comparison Worksheet (continued)

		Current Situation	What I want/ need	Loan Option A	Loan Option B
	Debt Accounts	**Balance**	**Monthly Minimum**		
9	Debt 1				
10	Debt 2				
11	Debt 3				
12	Debt 4				
13	Debt 5				
14	Debt 6				
15	Debt 7				
16	Debt 8				
17	**Total Debt (Total Line 9 through Line 16)**				
18	**Total Housing and Debt Expense**				
19	**Debt to Income Ratio (Line 18 / Line 1)**				

home (line 20), and enter the balance due on your present mortgage on line 26 (principal amount). The difference between these two lines is your equity (line 21). Compute your current LTV ratio (line 27) by dividing the balance due on your mortgage by the estimated value of your home. For example, if you estimate your home to be worth $300,000 and you currently owe $240,000 on your mortgage, your LTV ratio is $240,000 divided by $300,000 or 80 percent.

Then note your current lender's contact information on the form (lines 30 through 34), whether your current mortgage is a fixed rate or an adjustable rate (line 35), record the term (line 36), when it will be paid off (line 37) and the current interest rate (line 38). If your loan is subject to a prepayment penalty, note the amount of the penalty and when the penalty period expires on lines 39 and 40, respectively.

Table 7-1. Loan Comparison Worksheet (continued)

		Current Situation	What I want/ need	Loan Option A	Loan Option B
20	**Value of the home**				
21	Down payment or equity				
22	Balance owed on current mortgage				
23	Debt reduction amount				
24	Prepayment penalty				
25	Other cash out				
26	**Principal Amount**				
27	**Loan to Value Ratio (Line 26 / Line 20)**				
28	Minimum time in my home				
29	Minimum fixed payment period				

You now have a baseline against which to compare different options for a loan that meets your needs.

Table 7-1. Loan Comparison Worksheet (continued)

		Current Situation	What I want/ need	Loan Option A	Loan Option B
Offers					
30	**Lender Name**				
31	Contact				
32	Contact phone				
33	Contact email				
34	Contact FAX				
35	**Fixed or Adjustable?**				
36	**Term (years)**				
37	**Full Amortization Date**				
38	**Interest Rate (initial)**				
39	Prepayment penalty amount				
40	Prepayment penalty expiration date				

Navigating the Mortgage Minefield: Burying Your Head in the Sand Makes It Hard to Breathe

If you notice yourself resisting, avoiding, and dreading looking at and analyzing your current financial position as part of the process for responsibly obtaining a loan, know that you are not alone. It is human nature to avoid things that we fear will be unpleasant, whether that unpleasantness is real or imaginary.

No one can force or make you self-assess your financial position and goals. But to obtain a loan your past, present, and future financial situation will come under scrutiny by those who decide whether to lend you money. Are you going to hold your breathe, hoping that when the light shines on you that you won't be embarrassed or rejected for the loan? Or are you going to empower yourself to find out where you are so you know what direction you need to take to get to where you want to be financially?

Knowing where you want to get is not enough information to navigate safely there. You have to know your starting point. How do you get to Chicago? Whether you head east or head west depends on where you are starting from. Your financial situation is no different.

Many people fear that their financial situation is worse than it turns out to be, especially people who have never had to look at it before. You may be surprised and not be as bad off as you thought. Or things may be worse than you thought. It doesn't matter. They are what they are, and the most important thing is that you know what they are. And to know that if you don't like your situation, you have the power to alter it. Open your eyes, get into action, and take charge. You'll breathe a lot easier.

Describing What You Want

Now that you know where you stand financially, it is time to define where you want to go; what do you want to accomplish with your mortgage? Whether you are purchasing for the first time or refinancing, a good place to begin is to answer the question, "How much can I afford?" Assume your income will remain the same as it is today. Do you have enough discretionary money at the end of each month to increase your housing expense? Or do you need to reduce your monthly expenses to avoid more debt? Go into the mortgage transaction knowing the maximum monthly housing and debt expense you can carry and enter it at Total Housing and Debt Expense on your worksheet.

As a reality check, compute your debt to income ratio (line 19) based on your current income and the maximum monthly housing and debt payment you can handle. If the ratio is below 36 percent, you are on the right track for a conforming loan and decent terms. If the ratio is above 36 percent, compute the maximum amount of housing and debt expense that would give you a ratio of 36 percent by multiplying your gross monthly income by .36.

There are three ways that your new mortgage can deliver the monthly housing and debt expense you target: You can eliminate all your current debt and adjust your housing expense, you can retain all your current debt and adjust your housing expense, or you can reduce or eliminate a portion of your debt and alter both your housing expense and your monthly debt payments. This is the best point in your search for a mortgage to consider different options, so play with the numbers to see which of these three approaches provides the best solution for you and your family. We are going to create financing options A and B for the first and second situations, respectively.

Create Financing Options. Under Option A, if you eliminate all your monthly debt payments, the maximum housing expense you could carry would be the same as the maximum you computed that keeps your debt to income ratio at or below 36 percent. Under Option B, if you eliminate none of your monthly debt expense, the maximum housing expense you could carry is the difference between the maximum you computed for a 36 percent ratio and your total monthly debt payments. These two calculations define the limits of the range of housing expense you can afford.

For example, if your income is $8,000 per month, to keep your debt to income ratio at or below 36 percent, the maximum total you can afford is $8,000 × .36, or $2,880. In Option A, if your current monthly minimum debt payments total $500, and you eliminate all your debt, your maximum housing expense should be $2,880. Under Option B, if you pay off none of your debt, then your maximum housing expense should be $2,880 minus $500, or $2,380.

If you are going to eliminate or reduce your debt using the mortgage, you have to add the amount you want to pay off to the principal amount you are going to borrow. Total the debt balances and enter this figure on line 23 for Debt Reduction Amount under Option A. Enter zero on this line for Option B.

Loan to Value Calculations. Whether you are purchasing a home or refinancing, one of the factors that determines how much you can borrow is the value of your home. We are going to approach this section of the worksheet from two directions: If you are refinancing we will figure out the most money you can borrow, and if you are purchasing we will compute the maximum value of your new home.

If you are refinancing, enter your best estimate for the current market value of your home on line 20. Enter the principal balance remaining on your current mortgage and any second mortgages on line 22. Subtract the principal balances remaining from the estimated value of your home; this is the amount of your equity (line 21). Enter the amount of your prepayment penalty on line 24, if applicable. The total of your mortgage balances and prepayment penalty is the minimum amount of principal you will refinance. If this amount is greater than the estimated value of your home, you are "upside down" in your mortgage and will not be able to refinance until your principal balance comes down or real estate values go up.

Compute the LTV ratio as the minimum principal divided by the estimated value of your home. If the result is more than 80 percent, go back to the housing expenses and add PMI of .005 times the minimum principal, and recalculate your housing and debt numbers.

If you do not want to pay PMI, you can compute the maximum principal amount you can borrow that results in an LTV ratio of 80 percent by multiplying the estimated value of your home by .8. Next deduct the amount you owe on your current mortgages and any prepayment penalty, and the resulting number is the maximum you could have to pay off debt or cash out and avoid PMI. Once you know this number, you can modify the debt expense section of Options A and B and recalculate your debt and housing expenses and ratios.

If you are purchasing a home, how large a down payment are you able and willing to make (line 21)? To avoid PMI, compute the maximum loan amount by dividing your down payment by .2. Add this amount to your down payment to arrive at the maximum price of your new home. If you know you will be paying PMI, but you are not certain how much you want to borrow, go back to Chapter 2 to estimate the principal you can borrow based on your housing and debt to income ratios (including PMI), and remain within conforming loan guidelines. Add this amount to your down payment to arrive at the maximum value of a home you can afford.

Other Questions You Should Ask

What is the minimum length of time you plan to be in your home? The answer to this question will help you evaluate points, and whether a hybrid mortgage is an appropriate option for you.

What is the minimum period that you want your monthly payment to remain fixed? If you are open to a variable rate mortgage, you can mark this as zero time needed to remain fixed.

You now have a good idea of the parameters of the ideal loan for you. How you get there—what combination of interest rate, term, points, and closing costs meets the mark—is less important than whether the loan meets your requirements. Instead of trying to figure out whether the loan with more points is better than the loan with the higher interest rate, you can look at each option in terms of how well it meets your short- and long-term financial needs.

Calculating the Annual Percentage Rate

How do you know the real cost of financing when fees and costs vary? The Consumer Protection Act, passed by Congress in the 1960s, devised a way for consumers to obtain information about the cost of credit that allows them to compare credit offers. The Truth in Lending Act (TILA), which is part of the Consumer Protection Act, details the method for "equalizing" the cost of credit.

Basically, TILA deducts the fees and costs associated with obtaining credit from the amount of money being borrowed, so that the consumer can see the effective rate of interest, known as the *annual percentage rate (APR)*. Simply put, if you borrow $1,000 at an interest rate that results in a monthly payment of $100 (10 percent), and that $1,000 includes $200 of costs to obtain the credit, the APR tells you what interest rate on $800 borrowed results in a payment of $100 (12.317 percent). By using a formula that effectively converts the cost of credit to zero in all cases, you can compare offers and see which is more expensive. A higher APR indicates a higher cost of credit.

For example, if you borrow $100,000 at 6.5 percent interest for thirty years, and there are no closing costs or fees, then the APR is also 6.5 percent. Your monthly payment is $632.07. If you pay $2,800 in closing costs and fees, then the amount you are borrowing for the house is $100,000 less $2,800, or $92,700. The APR calculation answers the question "What percentage rate on the amount borrowed net of the costs and fees would result in the same payment as the stated interest rate?" The answer in this case is an APR of 6.768 percent. If you plug the net amount of $97,200 into a payment calculator, using thirty years and 6.768 percent with no costs, you will arrive at a monthly payment amount within a dollar of $632.07.

Beware of Advertised APR

When you shop online for mortgages, you will see the APR along with the interest rate. By law, any advertisement that states an interest rate must also state the APR. The conditions for which those APR calculations apply could be different from the conditions on your loan. For instance, the advertised APR may assume no PMI, or no extra charges for less-than-full documentation loans.

If you refinance or sell your home before the term ends (which most people do), then APR can mislead you. APR assumes the loan will exist for its full term, which means that up-front costs are spread over a long period. If the loan does not go to term, the APR is understated, and loans with higher up-front costs and lower interest rates could show a lower APR than loans with lower up-front costs and higher interest rates.

Compute Your Own Comparison

APR calculations are subject to interpretation, despite the intent of the law. The best way to compare the APR on different loan offers is to compute it yourself, consistently including or excluding the fees and costs about which you are aware.

You can use www.bankrate.com and navigate to "calculators" and "mortgages"; enter the amount and terms of your loan, the fees, points, and other costs associated with obtaining the credit; and compute the APR.

To compute APR for yourself, determine the "amount financed" for each loan offer that you consider. If the amount of your loan is $100,000, depending on each lender's costs and fees, the calculation of amount financed will be different. The TILA specifies the fees and costs deducted from the loan amount to arrive at the amount financed. It restricts the deductions to those items directly related to obtaining credit, and it specifically excludes costs that would be incurred even if the transaction involved no credit, such as filing fees and attorney fees.

If you are comparing offers from multiple lenders, you can apply the same principal to all the costs and fees associated with closing your mortgage. Ask for a detailed list of all costs, so you can compare things such as attorney fees, document prep fees, title fees, recording fees, and other fees that are all part of a real estate transaction, but which nonetheless may vary from lender to lender.

CHAPTER 8

SHOP FOR A PROVIDER
YOU CAN TRUST

Thirty years ago, if you wanted a mortgage you applied to your local banker who provided you with a fixed-rate mortgage at the prevailing interest rates. Today, you have choices that were unimaginable thirty years ago. Thanks to new technology, you have access to lenders across the nation without ever leaving your home. Using the Internet, you can compare rates, research mortgage products, and apply for a mortgage online without interacting with another human being. In addition, banks compete with brokers, wholesalers, and other lending institutions for your business, and the funds for your loan are more likely to come from Fannie Mae or Freddie Mac than from the deposits in your neighborhood bank. And fixed-rate mortgages, though still popular, are only one of many mortgage options available to you.

Today, the mortgage industry is among the most competitive there is; that's both the bad news and the good news. The mortgage industry is an easy one to enter, and when a steady stream of refinancing is fueled by low interest rates and high real estate values, many new mortgage companies enter the market. The bad news is that when economic conditions decline, many of those companies are unable to survive. The good news is that competition keeps costs low and stimulates the creation of new mortgage features and loan products, such as ARMs, hybrids, and interest-only loans. Regardless of the current economic conditions, the responsibility for choosing the loan provider and product that are right for you rests in your hands. With all those companies and products from which to choose, knowing how to select the right company with which to do business is more important than ever.

In this chapter you will learn:

☑ Who sells mortgages

☑ How to know whom you can trust

☑ What value-added services are available from providers

Who Sells Mortgages?

If you search the Internet for "mortgage" you will get hundreds of *millions* of results. How do you know whom to trust? The process you go through to obtain a loan will be the same whether you use a retail lender or use the services of a broker. You may not even know the difference by looking at the ads or talking with representatives. In the end, what is most important to you is service and a product that meets your financial needs.

Retail Lenders

The mortgage industry, like many others, has both retail and wholesale providers. Retail lenders, such as banks, savings and trusts, and credit unions, deal directly with borrowers like you.

When you walk into the branch of the bank where you do your personal banking, you will see advertising for home loans and lines of credit. Lenders employ people to take your application and discuss the loan products they offer. If you decide to move ahead, they will advance your application to another department to underwrite the loan, and finally to close and fund your loan.

Retail lenders have money available through the deposits of their customers. However, those funds are limited, and if they were the only source available, their money would be tied up for decades with each mortgage they funded. Very often retail lenders sell their mortgages on the secondary market to institutions like Fannie Mae and Freddie Mac, which means that their qualifying requirements will be comparable to those institutions.

Brokers

In addition to retail lenders, you can obtain a mortgage through a mortgage broker, who arranges transactions between borrowers and wholesale lenders for a fee. Wholesale lenders do not deal directly with borrowers, but instead depend on brokers to provide customer service and the initial screening and qualification. Brokers typically have close working relationships with many wholesale lenders. By familiarizing themselves with the lenders' products and qualifying guidelines they can save you the time and effort of shopping around for a loan that meets your needs.

If you want to do all the leg work yourself, you can do some comparison shopping armed with product information and questions you need to ask a lender about the proposed product. Just come up with a list of questions and create a side-by-side comparison of the answers that different lenders give you. Or you can save yourself some time and shop for a mortgage broker instead. Once you retain a broker, he or she will shop the market for you, and will bring his or her expertise to the analysis of the products available to you.

Brokers receive compensation for their services through brokerage fees, which are flat amounts or a percentage of the loan amount (points). They obtain funds for you at wholesale rates, mark up the price and sell to you at retail prices, much like any other business providing a service between wholesalers and end consumers. Wholesale lenders create complex pricing structures that offer different interest rates depending on the points, if any, that the borrower pays as part of the transaction. The interest rate at which no points are charged is called "par." In Chapter 6 you learned that by paying discount points at closing you effectively prepay interest on the loan and can obtain a lower interest rate and thereby reduce your monthly payment. The lower interest rate you get because of the discount points is "below par." Brokers add their fees, in the form of additional points, to the discount points quoted by the wholesaler when the broker gives you the price of the loan. The difference between the wholesaler's points for the agreed upon interest rate and the points you pay (from which the broker is compensated), is called the *yield spread premium*, and is disclosed in the application documents and the closing documents.

For example, if a wholesaler offers par pricing at 5.5 percent interest, and asks for a half point (0.5) to reduce the interest rate to 5.375 percent, and if the broker expects a 2 percent markup on the sale, the broker will quote you an interest rate of 5.375 percent with 2.5 points. The 2.5 points is the combination of the half point that the wholesale lender charges, and the 2 points for the broker's fee. At the closing you will pay the lender the 2.5 points, and then, outside of the closing, the lender will compensate the broker with the 2 points that were added as the markup. The 2 points paid by the lender to the broker outside of the closing is the yield spread premium.

In addition to below par pricing, wholesale lenders offer above par pricing, which is an interest rate that is higher than par, and for which the lender will rebate points to the broker. For example, if par is 5.5 percent interest, then if the broker sells the loan at 5.75 percent, the lender may rebate .875 points. If the broker is again looking for a 2 percent markup, the loan will be quoted to you as 5.75 percent with 1.125 points. The 1.125 points is the broker's 2 point markup less the .875 that the lender kicks in for the above par pricing. At closing you pay the 1.125 points, which will go to the broker, and outside of closing, the lender pays the other .875 as the yield spread premium to the broker.

Remember that wholesale lenders' rates are lower than those of retail lenders, and that retailers build their markup into the price of the loan. Retail lenders are not required to disclose the spread between their cost of funds and the rate they charge you. The yield spread premium and broker fees must be disclosed at the time of closing, but you may ask about them sooner. To complicate matters, some financial institutions perform the roles of both broker and lender. None of this is that important, as long as you understand with whom you are dealing, what they are providing, how much it is costing you, and whether is serves your needs.

Using the Internet to Find a Lender

There are many resources available to you on the Internet to find a mortgage. Many sites provide comparative rates, and many others give you information about mortgage products, the mortgage industry, and tips for getting through the process.

Use the Internet to shop around if you are not going to use a broker or a referral. But use it as a starting point, rather than as the final destination of your journey. At some point, you will deal with flesh and blood people, and the sooner you get a sense for how they operate and their level of professionalism and service, the better off you will be. Most sites have a way for you to contact the organization. Do that before you commit any money to them. Do they answer the phones? Do they return your calls? Is their e-mail response personal and prompt? If you are not getting exceptional service now, before you are a customer, don't expect miracles after you have put money into the game. Their behavior is likely to get worse, not better.

Many organizations allow you to complete online applications. Some request only enough information to pull a credit report before quoting you a rate. In any case, before you provide your social security number, bank accounts, or other sensitive and personal information, be certain that the site on which you enter that information is secure. Don't include this type of information in an e-mail, which is not protected. You can tell a secure website by a URL that begins with https:// rather than the usual http://.

When you make contact with an organization, start asking questions. How do people treat you? Are your questions answered and explained to your satisfaction? Do you trust the person?

Seller-Provided Direct Financing

When the real estate market is slow, sellers are more likely to provide financing to a buyer in order to move their house. A seller can "carry" the buyer's financing; the borrower directly pays the owner an agreed-upon amount of interest and principal each month.

What are the advantages to you, the buyer? If you are unable to qualify for a loan elsewhere, you may find an owner who will finance you. You and the owner negotiate the terms of an owner carry; you can have any terms and payment schedule upon which you mutually agree. You may be able to negotiate the down payment so that you do not have to come up with all the money at once, but make several smaller lump sum payments spread over time. There won't be closing costs associated with the owner carry, other than attorney fees, which we strongly recommend you pay to a lawyer to review the loan note for you.

What's in it for the owner? As an investment, the rate of interest you pay may be higher than the rate of return on other investments for which the seller could use the money. The seller may also be able to command a higher selling price because of the carry, since your choices may be more limited. In addition, your mortgage payment means a steady stream of income to the seller, and receiving payment over time may result in tax advantages for him or her.

What is the downside for you as the buyer with a seller carry? If the seller does not own the property outright, for instance he or she still owes a balance on their mortgage, and if the seller fails to make payment to his lender, your investment in the property is at risk.

Seller carry notes typically have a term of five to seven years. During this period, you have the opportunity to improve your credit and financial standing to be able to qualify for a mortgage with a traditional lender.

Who Should You Trust?

Sources for funds in the mortgage market are limited and competitive. As a result, you will find that the cost of funds does not vary greatly between lenders. From a product perspective, you have already learned that while there are numerous variations of the basic product, there isn't one mortgage "brand" that is better than another—money is money, and the terms are dependent on your financial state more than on the lenders' unique product offering. So, given that you can get the same basic product at the same basic price from pretty much any supplier in the market, to whom should you give your business?

As with any market where neither price nor product are distinctive, service is the factor by which competing companies can distinguish themselves. The mortgage companies that view themselves as providers of service are the ones that endure through the cyclical swings of the industry. They build their reputations on customer satisfaction, and build their business through referrals and returning customers. These companies are those with which you want to do business.

As with any important financial decision, you want to do business with people and institutions that you trust. You want to know that you are going to get what you expect, and that you can rely on the information provided to you by those you depend on. In the end, however, the person you most want to be able to trust is yourself. And the best way to do that is to be informed and be responsible; know what questions to ask and make sure you are satisfied with the answers you get. Assume nothing and question everything. When you operate that way, you quickly know whom you can trust to do business.

Mortgage Advertising

A mortgage is a product for sale. It has features, it has options, and it has marketing and sales presentations designed to get your attention and interest so you inquire further if you are a serious buyer. Take note of the fine print; you may not qualify for what is advertised, or it may cost you more than the advertised price.

To educate consumers, the Federal Trade Commission (FTC) issued a Consumer Alert on deceptive mortgage advertising. You can go to www.ftc.gov for the full text, but we'll cover some of the highlights here.

What ads leave out is as important as what they say. The FTC advises that certain phrases used in mortgage advertising should trigger questions. "Low fixed-rate" doesn't tell you for how long the rate is fixed. Remember that an ARM can have a fixed introductory rate that can last from one month to many years. Just because a rate is advertised as fixed, do not assume it means that it is fixed for the entire term of the loan.

"Low rates" can refer to interest rates, but can also refer to payment rates. Interest-only and minimum-payment option loans qualify as low payment rates, regardless of the rate of interest. Don't assume that the initial payment will remain the same over the term of the loan. With all mortgages other than a true fixed-rate, the payment fluctuates.

Similarly, "low payment amounts" could also refer to interest-only or minimum-payment options. Don't assume that the balance of the principal is paid in full during the term of the loan; balloon payment mortgages can have low payment amounts that catch up with you at the end of the term. "Pay only $$$ on loan amount of $$$$" should raise a red flag for introductory rates, interest-only, and minimum-payment options.

If you receive offers in the mail, be aware that many envelopes intentionally look as if they originate from your mortgage company or from the government. Your mortgage is a matter of public record, and the information about the amount, the timing, the interest rate, and the lender is collected and sold by list providers to mortgage originators to use in marketing campaigns. If the offer refers to eligibility for a government program and it looks like it comes from a government agency, check for the agency in the Blue Pages of your telephone book and call them to determine if the offer is legitimate.

Read the advertising fine print as well. Those **** and + + + symbols usually point to disclaimers about the feature being touted.

For example, one national lender's sponsored link on a popular search engine quoted "No Closing Cost Refi Options. No Points or Processing Fees. Call Now." However, at their website the fine print for the "No Closing Cost" option discloses that the closing costs are rolled into the financing and may result in a higher interest rate (not to mention a higher amount of principal refinanced). The same site advertises "low monthly payments"** where it warns that the number of payments and total amount may increase with refinancing, which would happen if you refinance by extending term, or if you make minimum or interest-only payments.

Referrals

Sources for loans are plentiful. How do you decide? One way is to ask someone you trust. If you have a friend, relative, or colleague who has had a positive mortgage experience, you can certainly ask for a referral. Your experience may not be the same as that of your friend, as your financial situation and goals may be very different. But if the referrer can attest to the level of service and general satisfaction with the way business was conducted, and if you are armed with the information you need about the questions to ask about the product being proposed, you have a good chance of getting a good deal and good service as well. Take advantage of the fact that you were referred—if the mortgage company blows it with you, they lose you and the person who referred you, plus all the business that that person will no longer refer.

If you are purchasing a home, your real estate agent or broker is a good source to refer a mortgage provider to you. By law, a mortgage professional cannot compensate a real estate broker or agent for referrals, and the real estate agent has an interest in your financing going smoothly.

Licensing and Regulation

Mortgage lenders and brokers are licensed in each state. *Mortgage News Daily*, an online mortgage trade publication, provides information about licensing requirements and governing bodies in each state at www.mortgagenewsdaily.com/mortgage_license. Be certain that the broker or lender with whom you are dealing is licensed to do business in the state in which the property exists.

You can also check with the Better Business Bureau at www .bbb.org to inquire about the company's reputation, whether complaints have been filed against it, and if so, how they were resolved. Only companies that are registered with the Better Business Bureau can display the bureau's seal.

Navigating the Mortgage Minefield: Corporate Values and an Ethical Compass

As with any costly purchase, you want assurances that the company with which you are doing business is reputable and that the individual upon whom you are relying for product information and advice is fully knowledgeable and ethical. How do you know? Here are some questions to ask to give you a sense of the company's values and its expertise.

☑ *How long has the company been in business?* It is easy to get into the mortgage business when interest rates are low and real estate values are high. It is hard to stay in the mortgage business when conditions turn and money becomes tight. A company that has endured through fat times and thin is one that has a solid base of clients and sound practices.

☑ *What experience and training does your representative have?* The only options that your loan originator can offer you are the ones about which he or she is aware and which he or she recognizes will make a difference for you. Training teaches originators about the products and the process. Experience teaches them

> where interpretation or judgment provides opportunities, and where there are dead ends that are not worth pursuing.
>
> ☑ *What percentage of the company's business comes from past customers and referrals?* The higher the number, the more emphasis the company places on long-term customer relationships, and that means service and a fair price.
>
> ☑ *How is the provider paid?* More important than the specific answer is the provider's willingness to be open and straightforward in response to your question. Compensation information is required to be disclosed to you in writing both at the time you submit your loan application, and when your loan closes, so if the provider is reluctant to disclose it, it probably is hoping you won't notice. Run!

Your Rights and Protections

The transactions involved in obtaining or granting a mortgage loan are governed by a number of bodies within the U.S. federal government. The laws require that loan documents disclose all the terms, conditions, and costs of the loan to the borrower. Provisions of the laws facilitate comparison of offers, and provide assurance of reputable practices.

This section identifies regulating bodies, highlights major rights and protections, and references sources of additional information for each step in obtaining a mortgage. In general, mortgage transactions are regulated and the rules enforced by the FTC's Bureau of Consumer Protection, which oversees credit transactions, and by HUD, which specifically deals with real estate transactions.

Fair Credit Reporting Act. The Fair Credit Reporting Act, enforced by the FTC, defines your rights with respect to credit reporting agencies or credit bureaus. Credit reporting agencies have a legal obligation to provide complete and accurate information, and to make available to you the information that creditors will use to determine whether to extend credit. They must make available to you annually, at no charge and at your request, a copy of your credit report, and must provide you with credit information provided to others who have denied you credit.

Protection Against Mortgage Discrimination. The Equal Credit Opportunity Act (ECOA) and the Fair Housing Act, both part of the Consumer Credit Protection Act enforced by the FTC, state that lenders cannot deny you credit on the basis of race or color, religion, national origin, gender, marital status, handicap, family status, age, receipt of public assistance, or the exercise of your rights under the Consumer Protection Act.

The law says that a lender cannot consider any of the previously stated conditions or attributes when evaluating your creditworthiness, the value of the property, or the value of your assets. This means that you have the same opportunity to obtain financing as anyone else with your financial status.

Real Estate Settlement Procedures Act. The Real Estate Settlement Procedures Act (RESPA) is an act of HUD. It is designed to inform you of all the details and costs associated with the transaction into which you are entering, and it specifies in detail not only the information that must be provided to you, but the documents you must sign to indicate that you received the required information.

RESPA comes into play at several points in the mortgage process. When your application is ready for underwriting, it requires the preparation and review of a Good Faith Estimate (GFE) document that details the anticipated costs associated with your loan. Chapter 10 contains more information about the Good Faith Estimate. The Mortgage Servicing Disclosure, also required by RESPA, tells you whether the lender will keep and service your loan, and how to resolve disputes.

Just prior to your closing, the closing agent prepares a HUD-1 Settlement Statement for you to review. Similar to the Good Faith

Estimate, the HUD-1 Settlement Statement requires detailed disclosure of all fees and costs associated with the loan. You must sign the HUD-1 Settlement statement at closing.

Additionally, RESPA requires disclosure of estimated escrow amounts on an Initial Escrow Statement. RESPA dictates that the organization that services your loan provides you with an annual escrow account statement, and when and how you receive notification if the party who services your loan is going to change.

Recourse. If you believe any party involved in your mortgage has violated your rights contact the governing body at one of the following:

Director, Interstate Land Sales/RESPA Division
Office of Consumer and Regulatory Affairs
U.S. Department of Housing and Urban Development
Room 9146
451 7th Street, SW,
Washington, DC 20410

Federal Trade Commission
Correspondence Branch,
Federal Trade Commission,
Washington, DC 20580

Services That Add Value to Your Mortgage Experience

As with any major purchase of a long-lasting product, you want to know that should you run into problems your concerns will be handled with great service. Some mortgage providers offer additional services to save you money by monitoring changes that can affect your loan or payments. Some of these services are offered for a fee. When you select a firm with which to do your mortgage business, ask which of the following services or products that you feel are valuable can be made available.

Accelerator Programs

In Chapter 6 we examined the impact of making accelerated payments on a long-term mortgage. By paying half the monthly payment every two weeks, you make the equivalent of thirteen payments per year instead of twelve, and pay off your thirty-year mortgage in about twenty-three years, saving substantial amounts of interest.

Many lenders offer accelerator programs. Some of them charge a one-time set-up fee. The way it works is that you pay them biweekly, and they accumulate your extra money until they can make an additional payment on your behalf. Ask whether the additional payment is applied entirely to reduce the principal, or whether a portion of it prepays interest. You can pay the loan off faster and pay less interest if all the extra payment is applied only to principal.

However, with some self-discipline you can implement your own accelerator program, avoid paying any fees, and earn interest on your money while it accumulates. You can accelerate in one of two ways: If you receive a biweekly paycheck, the easiest and most reliable way to accelerate your mortgage payment is to automatically withdraw half your monthly mortgage payment amount from your pay and deposit it into a savings account. Once a month pay your mortgage from the account. Every six months you will get an "extra" paycheck in a month. With your next mortgage payment, pay the additional half payment and designate it entirely for principal.

The second way you can implement your own accelerator program is to put aside each month an amount equal to one-twelfth of your monthly mortgage payment. Save that money in an account that you know you will not touch, and at the end of the year make an additional principal-only payment to your lender for the amount you have saved. If you cannot save that much each month, set aside what you can, and at the end of the year make a principal-only payment of the amount you have accumulated. No matter what amount you save and use in this way, you will cut time off your fixed-rate mortgage term and will save interest.

If you know you are not disciplined enough to avoid the temptation of spending that extra money elsewhere, consider the value of having a lender or broker perform the service for you. Even if it costs you a small amount in set-up fees or lost interest, you still make out better than if you don't do it at all.

Rate Watch/ARM Alerts

Interest rates fluctuate all the time. If you have a fixed-rate mortgage, refinancing can save you a lot of money when interest rates drop. Some lenders and brokers offer a service to track your interest rate against prevailing rates over time, and alert you when rates have changed enough for you to consider refinancing.

If you have an adjustable-rate mortgage, a rate-watch service is even more important to you. It gives you warnings about potential increases in rates that will affect your monthly payment, and it alerts you to opportunities to convert your ARM to a fixed-rate when interest rates are favorable.

A good rate-watch program also alerts you in advance to adjustment periods for your specific mortgage. In particular, with hybrids and ARMs with long introductory fixed rates, notification that your adjustment period is approaching reminds you to compare rates and look for opportunities to refinance and save money.

Position Improvement Programs

Some lenders and brokers offer programs designed to help you improve your credit and financial position so you can qualify for a loan or obtain better terms in the future. Many companies and individuals offer credit repair services, some for a fee, some free. If your broker or lender offers these services at no cost to you, you have the advantage of having someone working for you who knows your current financial situation and the current mortgage market conditions. If you start these services with someone new who is not familiar with your financial circumstances, or if you try to do it on your own without detailed knowledge of what is happening in the mortgage market, it may take you longer to get into a good mortgage, and you may miss opportunities that a professional who knows you would see.

There are steps you can take on your own at no cost to improve your credit scores, as described in Chapter 2. But credit is only one factor influencing your ability to obtain a mortgage. Some brokers offer cash flow guidance and support, investment advice, and other services to support you in reducing debt, increasing income, and accumulating a down payment.

New Product Alerts

An organization that values your business will stay in touch with you long after your mortgage closes. They will inform you of market conditions, provide tips to improve your home or your finances, and let you know about mortgage products that may be of interest to you.

Particularly with federal programs and specialized incentives from governmental agencies such as the Federal Housing Authority, HUD, and the Veteran's Administration, a good company informs you of new opportunities that become available and for which you may qualify. Local incentives and grant programs also undergo changes, and should be among the information provided to you by your mortgage provider.

Periodic Checkups

In line with fluctuating market conditions, new product offerings, and your changing financial situation, a company that values you as a customer will offer periodic checkups that compare your current mortgage with other options that may be available to you. These checkups should be free, as they stimulate business for the provider. There should be no obligation for you to do business, or do it with them, to get the checkup. Of course, if you have a provider looking for ways to save you money, why would you go elsewhere?

In order to perform a checkup, the provider may ask you to complete a mortgage application and for permission to obtain your credit report. With this information and your estimate of the value of your home, the provider should be able to determine whether you can save money by refinancing. You should not have to pay any fees for this service.

Regular Communication and Live Interaction

Do business with people who value you as a customer, not people who want to make a quick buck on a single transaction. When you deal with an organization that has a strategy for staying in communication with you and for making available to you experts who can answer your questions at any time, then you know you are dealing with people who are not going to jack up the cost of your mortgage. They are interested in having you return as a customer, and want you to refer to them your friends, family, neighbors, and colleagues when they have mortgage questions or mortgage needs.

CHAPTER 9

TAKE CHARGE OF THE LOAN APPLICATION PROCESS

When you understand the loan application process, you have control. When others see that you are an informed, active participant, they will respond to meet your expectations for accurate and timely information and the excellent service that you deserve.

Completing the application with you is a way for the loan originator to learn about your financial position and your goals so that he or she can recommend the right mortgage product to meet your needs. The information you provide for the application and in conversations with the loan originator, and the ease and accuracy with which you provide it, tell the loan originator how responsible, informed, and committed you are. The originator can then tailor the discussions with you so that you fully understand the choices available to you, and are ready to submit your loan application and supporting documents to the lender.

The loan application package contains the income, debt, credit, and property information that a lender must have to determine whether to lend you money and with what terms. After you have submitted your application, an underwriter assesses your creditworthiness and decides whether to grant you the mortgage. It is not unusual for the lender to request additional information or documentation from you in order to approve your loan. Then, assuming your loan is approved, steps are taken to arrange a closing.

In this chapter you will learn:

☑ What questions you must answer on the mortgage application and why they are asked

☑ What fees you must pay

☑ What the Good Faith Estimate tells you about your proposed mortgage

☑ What happens after your application is approved

The Uniform Residential Loan Application

Fannie Mae and Freddie Mac use the Uniform Residential Loan Application to accept information about borrowers. If the loan originator with whom you are working is experienced, he or she will use the application to learn about you, your family, and your goals. If the application is not used in this way, the originator will be unable to recommend a mortgage package that meets your needs. In addition, the application process helps you understand your financial situation and determine what you want from your mortgage. The process of completing the application may take more than one conversation between you and the originator, because a good originator will want to establish a relationship with you and earn your trust, and that takes more than one interaction. The interactions should be more like a conversation in which you are getting to know each other than an interrogation to fill in the application form, and if they are not, consider finding another originator who relates to you as a person rather than as a sale.

The application form, referred to as the 1003 (pronounced ten-oh-three), has many sections. For your loan to progress smoothly, the application information you provide must be complete and accurate. As you answer the questions, be sure that the information is recorded properly by spelling out for the originator the names of streets, employers, and similar information.

Borrower Information

The application asks for information about you, such as your social security number and date of birth, that is needed to request your credit report from a credit agency or credit bureau. Your name must appear on the application in exactly the form you want it to appear on all the legal documents pertaining to the mortgage. The mortgage note, deed, and all supporting documentation will use the form of your name entered with the application, whether with a middle initial or without one, followed by Jr. or other similar designation.

The mortgage originator will ask for your home phone number, work number, and mobile phone number. Let him or her know which is the best number to reach you, and the best times to call; at some point in the process it is likely that he or she will need to reach you—for example, to request additional information or documentation—and the easier you are to reach, the faster the process will go.

The application also requires information about where you have lived for the past two years, and if you have not lived at your current address for at least two years, you will have to provide previous addresses. This information helps ensure that the lender sees complete mortgage or rent payment history on your credit report.

The originator will ask about your marital status and family as well, including the age of your children and any other dependents. While this information is required on the application, it serves the additional purpose of giving the originator a sense of your longer-term financial requirements. If you are just starting a family, your needs will be different than those of a family with children about to enter college, or those of a family whose children are grown and self-sufficient. If you do not feel comfortable discussing these things with the loan originator, or if the originator does not inquire about financial plans centered on your family situation, again, consider changing originators. Remember that a good mortgage professional not only knows the details of current mortgage products, but knows how to match your needs with the product that will best meet your short- and long-term financial needs.

Employment Information

Your employment history is an important indicator of the stability of your income. Because lenders are more interested in your ability to pay your mortgage than in foreclosing on your home if you cannot, they not only assess the likelihood that you will retain your present employment position, but also the likelihood that you will be able to secure another job in your field of expertise, should you lose your current position.

Employment history going back at least two years is required. You provide the company name, address, the dates you worked there, and how much money you made at each position in the last two years, and the lender will contact your employers to verify the information you have provided, unless you apply for a no-documentation or no-verification loan.

A history of job-jumping, even within the same field, raises a red flag for the lender about your ability to keep a job and maintain a steady income flow. If you recently changed companies but remained in the same field of work, it won't hurt you. If you've changed jobs several times due to circumstances that were not a result of your performance or your choice to leave, it should be noted on the application by the loan originator.

Self-Employed Borrowers. If you are self-employed, own a business, or earn all your income as an independent contractor, you are a higher risk to lenders than someone who is employed in a full-time job. If you have been in business for less than two years, qualifying for a loan can be difficult.

If you recently transitioned from employment at a job to being self-employed, again, this should be noted by your originator. Some circumstances offset the risk if you've been in business for less than two years; for example, if your business is in the same industry in which you were employed, or if you have completed an educational program to enter your current field.

Income

The next section of the Uniform Residential Loan Application requests information about your income and monthly housing expense. The amount of money you make (or made at previous positions) is less important than your earning trend (such as whether your income is growing or shrinking), and how your income compares with your expenses (your housing ratio and debt to income ratio).

If you have a job, you must specify your gross monthly income. If your income varies because of overtime, tips, commissions, and bonuses, you can compute your monthly gross income as an average of your total earnings for the past two years.

Unless a large portion of your income comes from other sources, such as interest, dividends, alimony, child support, public assistance, or rental income, you do not have to include it. However, the higher the income you include, the better your housing ratio and debt to income ratio are, which means the more favorable rates. If a sizable portion of your income is from one or more of these sources, or if you depend on that income to meet your monthly expenses, include it.

Self-Employed Borrowers. Lenders calculate your housing and debt to income ratios based on the net taxable income that you report on your tax returns. As a self-employed person or business owner, you may take advantage of tax deductions that reduce your net taxable income, and which result in poorer housing and debt to income ratios. Consider a no-income documentation loan that allows you to state your gross income for use in ratio calculations. It will cost a fraction of a point in additional interest rate to use the stated income alternative, but it could result in better terms than those available to you based on your net taxable income.

Rental Income. If you own property from which you receive rental income, and you want that income included in your income qualification, advise your loan originator. Lenders consider only "net rental income," not the amount you collect in rent, which is called "gross rental income." When computing net rental income, only 75 percent of the rent you collect counts, and the mortgage principal and interest, taxes, and insurance you pay on that property are deducted from that figure. For example, if you collect $800 per month in rent, and the monthly mortgage principal and interest are $400, and the taxes and insurance are another $100, then the net rental income is ($800 $\times$ .75) − (400 + 100), or $60 per month.

Housing Expense

The lender will also ask about your current housing expense and your anticipated housing expense, based on the mortgage for which you are applying. If you currently rent, your housing expense is your monthly rent and renter's insurance. Once you have a mortgage and if you are refinancing your home, your housing expense includes your monthly mortgage principal and interest, as well as hazard insurance, real estate taxes, PMI, and any condominium or co-op association fees. If you presently own a home and these items are part of your escrowed funds, they appear on your monthly mortgage statement. If you pay these bills directly, find the amounts from the bills you received in the past year.

The lender wants your housing expense for the new mortgage to be 28 percent or less of your monthly income. A higher percentage will result in a less favorable interest rate, or denial of your application.

Assets

Additionally, the lender will want to know how long your savings could cover your housing expense if your income stream is interrupted. Two months of reserves is sufficient for borrowers with good credit. A six-month reserve helps if your credit is not great. Your reserve is the sum of your savings account balances, checking account balances, and 70 percent of your vested retirement funds. If you own a business, include your estimate of the value of your business in your asset calculation.

If you are purchasing a home, the source of funds for the down payment is of interest to the lender. If the down payment comes from your savings or other asset accounts, those funds are excluded when the lender calculates your reserves.

You must provide several months of statements showing the balances of your asset accounts, unless you apply for a no-asset verification loan. Large recent increases in assets raise questions; the lender wants assurance that your assets haven't increased temporarily just to obtain a loan. If you have accumulated your assets by saving over time, it tells the lender you have good financial habits, and this is more favorable than if you inherited a sum of money or were awarded a legal judgment.

If you are refinancing, include the estimated value of your home as an asset. Your real estate tax bill tells you how your town valued your property for your tax assessment. Check with the taxing authority (city or state) to learn what percentage of market value your assessment is, and use it to calculate the estimated value of your home. For example, if your tax bill shows an assessment of $140,000 and your town's assessment is 70 percent of fair market value, then the estimated value of your home is $140,000/.70, or $200,000.

The value of your home will be determined by the appraisal prior to underwriting.

Declarations

The lender is interested in retaining its security interest in the mortgaged property, and in your ability to meet the monthly payments. A series of questions at the end of the loan application will identify any potential problems about which the lender should be concerned. The questions uncover any potential outside claims on your assets, including the property securing the requested mortgage, and whether you meet your financial obligations. You state whether there are any outstanding judgments against you, such as collections, or garnishing of your wages to repay a debt. The application asks whether you have declared bankruptcy within the last seven years, if you ever have been foreclosed upon, or were forced to give over a deed or title on property or other loans, and if you are a party to a lawsuit. The lender also wants to know if you currently are in default on any loans. If you answer "yes" to any of these declarations, provide a written explanation.

The application asks about your citizenship, whether you will occupy the mortgaged property as your primary residence, and if you have owned a home in the last three years to determine your qualification for federal first-time home-buyer programs.

The Next Steps in the Loan Application Process

When you complete the application, the loan originator pulls your credit report, which provides your credit score and information about your debt and your credit history. A good mortgage originator takes the time to review your credit report and credit score with you, asks you questions, and answers any questions you may have. The loan originator should present you with options based on the type of mortgage for which you are likely to qualify, and the terms you are likely to pay.

Once you have settled on the kind of mortgage that meets your needs, an application fee of several hundred dollars may be required to proceed. The application fee covers some of the costs to prepare the loan application package for submission to the lender, and signals to the originator that you are serious about obtaining financing through him or her. Some brokers and lenders refund or credit the application fee when the loan closes.

The loan application package consists of your loan application, credit report, documents that support your statements of income and assets (unless you've opted for a no-documentation or no-verification loan), and a slew of legal forms and documents designed to fully inform you of the details of the transaction into which you are about to enter.

Good Faith Estimate

An additional document, required by RESPA, is the Good Faith Estimate (GFE). The GFE informs you of the fees and costs associated with obtaining the loan. Although the originator must provide you with the GFE within three days of submitting the application, you can request this document in advance. If you have questions about any of the items that appear on the GFE, ask the originator to explain them to you. Do not stop asking questions until you are satisfied that you understand the answers. It is your money.

The GFE also lists a number of fees. The *loan origination fee* is the fee or points that the lender charges to process the application. The *loan discount* is the additional percentage points you agree to pay in exchange for a lower interest rate. Listed as well in the GFE are appraisal fees, credit report fees, inspection fees, and mortgage insurance application fees.

Title insurance, title search fees, and transfer fees are itemized, as are recording fees and any other fees associated with obtaining the mortgage.

In most cases, your first mortgage payment will not be due until at least thirty days after the closing. The interest that accrues between the closing and the first mortgage payment is paid in advance at the closing, and is itemized on the GFE.

If you are purchasing a home, the GFE itemizes advance payments due to third parties, such as insurance premiums, PMI, and real estate taxes.

The yield spread premium represents a fee the lender pays to a broker outside of the closing. Typical broker compensation varies up to 4 percent of the amount of the loan.

What Happens Behind the Scenes

Once you sign all the documents in the loan package, the originator requests an appraisal and holds your file pending the appraisal report. When the appraisal arrives, the originator lets you know whether the appraised value of your home is close to the estimate on the application. If the appraised value is significantly less than the estimated value, the originator-proposed loan may be reworked. If the LTV ratio based on the appraisal is lower than 80 percent, you will have to pay PMI, which will also affect your housing and debt to income ratios.

If your appraisal is not significantly different from your estimate, the originator submits your loan application package to a lender for underwriting. The underwriter reviews all the information, and may ask for additional documentation or state other conditions which you must meet in order for the loan to be approved. It is important to respond quickly to the requests for additional information. Market conditions change all the time, so the faster your application is processed, the more likely it is that the terms of the approved loan will closely match the terms you expected based on the application.

If the lender approves your application, the originator informs you of the terms, including the interest rate, monthly payment, PMI, escrow, and other fees and costs. Note that the lender reserves the right to adjust interest rates at the time of closing, which could result in a different payment than you are expecting. However, you can pay a small fee to lock the approval rate until the closing. You can even pay for a rate lock that protects you against interest rate increases, but allows a decrease in your rate if interest rates drop. This "float down" rate lock is a good option when interest rates are volatile.

Although rate locks protect you against rate increases, they do have expiration dates and are very expensive to extend. If you purchase a rate lock, know when it expires, and manage the process to ensure that you close before the lock does.

Navigating the Mortgage Minefield: What to Do If Your Loan Application Is Denied

It is natural to be disappointed if your application for a mortgage is denied. Don't give up! Just because one lender said no doesn't mean no one will ever say yes. While it may be a setback, being turned down doesn't mean the end of your hopes and plans for the future.

By law, if a lender rejects your request for a loan, it must notify you in writing, and specify the reason for which you were denied credit. If the reason is worded in a general way, it doesn't tell you what you need to do to get approval in the future. Ask your mortgage originator or lender for specific information that will identify the areas you must improve to win their approval in the future.

There is enough variation in underwriting guidelines among lending institutions that rejection by one doesn't mean another lender won't approve you, based on the same application. If your LTV, housing ratio, debt to income ratio, or credit score are borderline with one lender, you may be within approval guidelines with another.

If you are denied by a retail lender, consider going to a mortgage broker for a second opinion. Bring all your documents with you, including the letter of denial. Because brokers have relationships with many lenders and are familiar with their underwriting guidelines and policies, they may be able to submit your application to a lender who will accept your current financial status as is. A broker will also know if you qualify for government-insured loan programs, such as those offered by the FHA or VA, which have less stringent qualification requirements.

If you cannot get funding based on your current circumstances, start taking steps to improve the areas of your financial profile that were unacceptable. Over time, you can improve your credit score, save money to increase reserves or down payment, pay down or eliminate debt, and even increase your income. Reapply in four to six months if you have been able to make improvements in the areas that caused you to be denied.

While you are making the needed changes to improve your credit-worthiness, you can begin enjoying the lifestyle of home ownership through *rent-option-to-buy* programs. These programs put you into a house as a renter for a limited period of time, after which you have an option to buy the home at a price specified at the time you sign the rental agreement. This arrangement gives you time to get your finances in order to be able to qualify for a mortgage when it is time for you to exercise your option to buy. Visit www.tomortgageservices.com for more information about rent-option-to-buy and credit repair services.

Finally, your broker or lender will schedule a closing date for you. Depending on the laws of the state in which the property resides, you may need an attorney to review the closing documents and represent you at the closing.

When you take charge of the application process, you protect yourself against errors, misrepresentation, and misunderstandings. You have control of your financial future.

CHAPTER 10

UNDERSTAND YOUR
INSURANCE OBLIGATIONS

When you get a mortgage, you assume obligations to purchase certain types of insurance. Let's be clear about who the insurance protects. Any insurance required by the lender protects that lender against your default as well as from declining property values. While some of the insurance may protect you as well, the obligation is not expressly for your benefit.

In this chapter you will learn:

☑ What conditions require PMI, how long you must pay it, and how you can end it

☑ What levels of home owner's or hazard insurance protect you and the lender

☑ What conditions require flood insurance or other hazard insurance

☑ What title insurance is and who it protects

☑ What credit life insurance is and who it protects

Private Mortgage Insurance

As discussed earlier in this book, Private Mortgage Insurance (PMI) protects the lender if you default on your mortgage. That may sound one-sided, but when you have less than 20 percent equity in your home PMI protects the lender's security interest in your property. The theory is that the more investment you have in your home, the less likely you are to default, and the larger the cushion between the amount of your loan and the value of your property if you must sell in a declining real estate market. PMI, by lessening lender risk, allows people to buy homes without having to accumulate large sums of cash for a down payment. With a down payment of as little as 3 percent, you can still qualify for a loan, as long as you pay PMI. Regardless of credit or income ratios, every borrower who does not have a 20 percent down payment or 20 percent equity in their home must pay PMI.

If you have to pay PMI, the lender adds the cost of the insurance to your monthly mortgage principal and interest payment, and then works with a mortgage insurance company to provide the coverage. If you default and your property goes into foreclosure, the insurance provider pays the lender an agreed-upon percentage of the mortgage to cover the costs of filing a foreclosure against you. Typical percentages for conforming loans are about .5 percent; the percentage charged for nonconforming loans may be higher.

Conditions Under Which PMI Can Be Cancelled

In 1999, the U.S. government passed the Homeowner's Protection Act, which specifies conditions under which a lender must terminate PMI for loans that closed after July 29, 1999. It also specifies limited circumstances under which the insurance company must automatically cancel the insurance.

Under the Homeowner's Protection Act you can request, in writing, the cancellation of PMI. The lender must comply if (a) your principal balance falls below 80 percent of the original value of the house (as determined by the appraisal), (b) you have no other liens on the property, (c) you have a good payment history, and (d) the value of the property has not declined. If the lender denies your request, it must inform you of the reason.

If you have to pay PMI, the lender must notify you in writing at the closing. The lender must also inform you of the terms and procedures for cancellation of the insurance. It pays to keep this document where you can refer to it, because you will want to know when and how you are able to request cancellation.

How do you know when you are eligible to request cancellation of PMI? The first thing is to know when the principal balance on your loan falls below 80 percent of the original value of the home. When you close the loan, make a note of the value of the home as indicated by the appraisal, and then follow your outstanding loan balance on your mortgage statement. Then, when you think you may qualify for cancellation, calculate the 20 percent equity you must have by multiplying the appraised value times 20 percent. Next, subtract that amount from the appraised value to determine the principal balance at which you may qualify for cancellation, and compare it to the balance you owe on your mortgage to see if you are close.

For example, if you borrow $195,000 to finance a home appraised at $200,000 then for you to have a 20 percent equity interest in your home, your equity has to reach $40,000 ($200,000 × .20 = $40,000). When your principal balance, as reported on your mortgage statement, reaches $160,000 ($200,000 − $40,000), you will have sufficient equity to qualify for cancellation, as long as you meet all the other cancellation criteria.

In addition to sufficient equity, another criterion to qualify for cancellation of PMI is that the property value has not declined since the time of the loan. If property values decline significantly, your equity percentage shrinks, because the principal balance represents a higher percentage of the current value of the home. If you suspect values have declined, request a free market analysis from a real estate agent or broker to get a ballpark value for your home. Then compare this estimate to the principal balance to determine if you are near the 20 percent mark. If so, expect to pay for a formal appraisal before the lender agrees to cancel the PMI. The appraisal costs several hundred dollars, so be certain that your lender will consider cancellation before committing to the appraisal.

While declining property values hinder your ability to cancel PMI, unfortunately, rising values do not help you. However, if property values increase significantly, consider refinancing for terms that improve your situation and eliminate PMI.

Another Form of Mortgage Insurance: FHA Loans

The Federal Housing Authority insures FHA mortgages and protects the lender if you default. If the lender forecloses, the FHA buys the house and resells it. Although the government insures the loan, you pay the *mortgage insurance premium (MIP)*. Beginning in June 2008 the FHA implemented risk-based MIPs, meaning the higher your LTV and the lower your credit score, the higher the MIP. You pay the MIP fee up front as a percentage of the principal you borrow, and it ranges from 1.25 percent to 2.25 percent. The fee is added to the amount of the loan, so while you don't have to pay it all at once, you pay interest on it over the term of the loan.

In addition to MIP, FHA loans also require that you pay a monthly insurance fee. As with MIP, as of June 2008 the amount you pay is determined based on risk, as reflected in your LTV and credit score. The insurance ranges from .50 percent to .55 percent of the base amount of the loan, which is determined by a complex set of rules and calculations.

If you prepay your FHA loan, you may request a prorated refund of your up-front insurance payment. The refund must be requested, though; it is not automatic. The Homeowner's Protection Act specifically excludes FHA loans, and the FHA is under no obligation to notify you of your right to this partial refund.

Hazard Insurance

In addition to PMI, your lender requires you to obtain and maintain insurance that protects you and the lender in cases where your home is damaged or destroyed by hazards such as fire, storm, flood, or earthquake. The lender specifies the amount for which you must insure your home, based on the home's value and the loan amount, and you must provide proof at the closing that the insurance is in effect.

In most cases, your lender will allow you to select the insurer from whom you obtain coverage, because most hazards (with the specific exceptions of flood and earthquake) are typically covered within a more comprehensive home owner's insurance policy that you would typically carry. Shop around for insurance providers. Most insurance providers offer a discount if you insure both your home and your automobiles with them.

Homeowner's Insurance

A standard homeowner's insurance policy insures your home against damage caused by disasters like fire, storm, and lightning. The coverage pays to repair or rebuild all or part of your home, and usually includes other structures on your property that are detached from your house, such as detached garages, tool sheds, and gazebos. Plants, shrubs, and trees are also covered for certain disasters, including theft, fire, lightning, vandalism, and explosions, but typically not for damage caused by wind or disease.

Most homeowner's policies also include payment for living expenses if you are unable to remain in your home during the repair of damages resulting from disasters covered by your policy.

Note that structural damage caused by flood, earthquake, or poor maintenance is specifically excluded from typical homeowner policies. The policies do not cover maintenance or repair of things that cause damage, only the damage caused. For example, if you take reasonable care of your roof, but nonetheless it leaks and causes water damage to the contents of your home, your homeowner's policy may cover the damage to the contents of your home, but it will not cover the repair of the roof.

A typical homeowner's policy also insures most items in your home—such as furniture, appliances, computers, decorations, and clothing—against destruction or theft both on the premises of your home and off premises. Expensive items such as jewelry or furs are typically covered to a very limited extent, but additional coverage specifically for these items is obtainable at an additional cost.

In addition to structural damage to your home and its contents, homeowner's insurance typically covers your liability for damages or injury to others, or to the property of others, caused by you or members of your family, including pets. Note that the damage or injury must be to *others* to be covered under the liability portion of your homeowner's policy; if your pet destroys *your* furniture, the liability insurance under your homeowner's policy will not cover it, but if your pet does the same damage to your neighbor's belongings, it will. Most homeowner's policies include medical coverage for people injured on your property, excluding you, your family, or your pets, as well.

Your lender dictates the amount of hazard insurance coverage you must maintain. All other components of a typical homeowner's policy are at your discretion. It pays to shop, as coverage options and costs can vary considerably.

Navigating the Mortgage Minefield: Why Your Credit Score Matters to Insurers

Did you know that your credit score affects the amount of your homeowner's insurance premium? It does. Before issuing you a policy, the insurance company will compute your "insurance score," which is based in part on the same credit score used by your mortgage lender.

Homeowner's insurance policy pricing is based on risk, just as mortgage pricing is. The greater the risk that you will file a claim against your policy, the more you will pay for insurance. Statistical studies used for pricing insurance show that how you manage your finances is a good predictor of the likelihood that you will file an insurance claim. People who handle financial matters well are statistically less likely to file an insurance claim than people who do not manage their finances well. Your credit score reflects how well you handle your finances, and the better your credit score, the less likely you are to file a claim. A solid credit history and credit score give you a high insurance score, and reduce the premium you pay for your homeowner's insurance.

Condos and Co-ops

If you are purchasing a condominium or a co-operative apartment, you may need additional hazard and liability insurance to cover your share of common areas in your building, such as the roof, basement, walkways, and elevators. Responsibility for insurance covering shared structures usually rests with the condominium association or co-op board, but you will pay a share of the cost. Sometimes the association is responsible for insuring all or part of the structure or content of individual units. For example, the association may insure the walls, floors, and ceilings of each unit, but nothing else. Or, included with the association's coverage for your unit may be coverage for fixtures and appliances that came with the unit, such as cabinets, plumbing, or bathroom fixtures. Contact your association and read your association's bylaws to know specifically the areas and structures for which you are personally responsible, because it is for these items that you should get insurance.

Flood and Earthquake Insurance

Although most homeowner's policies specifically exclude coverage for damage from floods and earthquakes, flood insurance can be purchased through private insurers. This insurance is backed by FEMA through a program called FloodSmart. FEMA sets the rates for flood insurance, so it doesn't matter from whom you obtain it, and it has maps of every part of the country on which it designates high-risk and moderate-to-low-risk flood plains. If your property is in a high-risk flood plain, your mortgage lender will require that you purchase flood insurance. However, even if your property is not in a high-risk area, you can obtain this insurance if it makes you feel more secure. Flood insurance protects your home, its contents, and other buildings on your property against losses caused by rain, coastal storm surge, melting snow, blocked storm drainage systems, and levee dam failure, but it does not protect against damage to the land.

FEMA advises that even a few inches of flooding can cause thousands of dollars of damage. You can purchase flood insurance for properties outside of high-risk areas for as little as $119 per year. A quarter of all flood insurance claims come from low-to-moderate risk areas affected by large floods.

If you live in an area that has a high risk of earthquakes, (go to www.fema.gov/hazard/earthquake/risk.shtm to see how your state ranks), consider buying an earthquake insurance policy. Again, as with flood damage, most standard homeowner's policies specifically exclude damage from earthquakes. Since the damage from an earthquake can mean a total loss of your home, the question to ask if you have equity in your home is "could I afford to rebuild?" If your home is destroyed, you still owe the balance of your mortgage.

Earthquake insurance is expensive, and the deductibles are high, and generally are a percentage of the value of the home. If you are considering buying a home in an earthquake area, look for the "retrofitting" features of the home, such as a braced water heater, "sheer" panels to reinforce walls, and a house frame that is bolted to the foundation. These features will reduce the damage caused by an earthquake, but are not a substitute for earthquake insurance.

Title Insurance

Title refers to the rights in a piece of property. It also refers to a document that serves as evidence of ownership and is transferred from one party to another to complete the transfer of ownership, such as in a sale. In most countries with sophisticated real property laws, such as the United States, title documents are registered with local governing bodies, where they become public records and are accessible by anyone who wants to see them. By researching the title transfers for a property, the title search identifies and verifies the "chain of title."

Part of the title information includes liens against the property, such as mortgages and unpaid real estate taxes. These liens represent a secured interest in the property, and generally prevent its transfer until the lien is released, which is usually through payment of the

debt. If through an error or deception a property transferred ownership with an outstanding lien against it, the chain of title for that
property is not considered "clean" because the lien holders still have
a right in the property, unknown to the buyer. A mortgage lender
requires a title search, whether for a purchase or a refinance, to determine whether the chain of title is clean.

The lender obtains, but the borrower pays for title insurance. The
insurance protects the lender in the event that the title search misses
something, as well as against claims and legal fees that arise should
an interest holder in the property press a claim. As part of the closing
costs on your mortgage, you pay a one-time title insurance fee in
addition to the title search fee. Each item is listed on both the Good
Faith Estimate at the time of the application, and on the HUD-1 Settlement Statement at the closing.

The required title insurance covers the lender for the loan amount,
but does not cover your equity in the home. You can purchase coverage on your own.

Unlike other types of insurance, title insurance covers events that
occurred in the past, up until the day the policy is issued. That is why
even a refinance transaction requires a title search and title insurance,
specifically to determine that nothing has affected the title since the
last transaction. If you failed to pay your real estate taxes, or if you
used the equity in your home to secure a personal loan, the title
search should uncover it, but if it misses, title insurance will protect
the lender.

Credit Life Insurance

Credit life insurance protects the lender for the balance of the loan in
the event of your death, ensuring that the mortgage will be paid off.

Related to credit life is *credit disability insurance,* which protects the lender for the balance of the loan in the event you are disabled and unable to pay the mortgage.

According to the Office of the Comptroller of the Currency, a lender cannot require credit life nor credit disability insurance, and must disclose the cost if it is included in the transaction or the monthly mortgage payment. Once it is part of the monthly payment, it is part of your agreement with the lender, so if it is included, be certain you are informed of the means by which you may cancel it.

CHAPTER 11

READ THE FINE PRINT
BEFORE CLOSING

Whether you are purchasing your first home, moving, or refinancing your home, once a lender approves your loan you'll look forward to the closing, which legally completes the transaction. For many people, the closing is a mysterious legal meeting at which they simply "sign here" when told to do so by an attorney or other closing agent. We want you to know and understand the documents and disclosures you will sign.

In this chapter you will learn:

☑ What happens at the closing

☑ How to read and understand a HUD-1 Settlement Statement

☑ What the fine print of your mortgage note means

☑ What you need to know about the mortgage deed

☑ What other documents you will sign at closing, and what they mean

What Happens at the Closing

The *closing* is a meeting where you, the lender, and, if you are buying a home, the seller, sign documents related to the property, the transfer of property ownership, the mortgage note, and the mortgage transaction. It is presided over by a closing agent, who may be an attorney, depending on state law. When you buy a home, the closing marks the transfer of property ownership, and the placement of the lender's lien on the property in accordance with the final mortgage agreement. If you are refinancing rather than purchasing a home, then no transfer of ownership takes place at the closing. However, the closing results in the repayment of your old mortgage and the removal of your previous lender's lien on your property, and the placement of a new lien on the property by the new lender. After the closing, the documents conveying the change of ownership and/or lien holders for the property are filed by the closing agent with the appropriate governing body (for example, your town's clerk). Once filed, they become part of the public record.

If you are purchasing a home, you take possession of and get the keys to your new home at the end of the closing. If you are renting, schedule the closing near the end of your lease. If that is not possible, negotiate with your landlord to let you sublease or to release you from the lease to avoid paying both rent and mortgage for any length of time. The timing of your closing, particularly if you are selling one home and buying another (and the seller is doing the same), requires planning and coordination so that you don't find yourself either with two houses or with no house for any time.

If you are moving, and your new home needs work such as painting, carpentry, or repairs that you want completed before you move in, schedule the closing in advance of the move, as work cannot begin until you take ownership of the property. If you are moving in on the same day as the closing, schedule the closing in the morning and the move in the afternoon, as you will not be able to move your belongings in until the closing is complete and the house is officially yours.

Schedule your closing at a time when you can devote several hours of attention to it. If it goes smoothly, it will take only about an hour, but leave extra time in case questions or other circumstances take longer than expected.

Reading and Understanding a HUD-1 Settlement Statement

The HUD-1 Settlement Statement, required by RESPA, is important to review and understand before the closing because it contains all the financial details about the mortgage and the property transfer for both the buyer and the seller. If the mortgage is a refinance, the HUD-1 shows only buyer information. It includes the costs and fees associated with the mortgage financing, and the amount of money you will either have to bring to the closing, or the amount of money you will receive following the closing.

If you have navigated through the mortgage minefield as recommended up to this point, you are already familiar with the GFE, which was one of the documents you signed at the time your mortgage originator submitted the application to the lender for approval. The GFE is similar in both form and content to the HUD-1 Settlement Statement, and serves as a preview to the HUD-1 Settlement Statement.

One section of the HUD-1 that merits explanation here is the settlement between the buyer and seller. This section details the cost of items for which the seller has paid, but which the buyer receives with the ownership of the home. For example, heating oil is often specified as an item of settlement between the buyer and seller; if the seller fills the heating oil tank prior to the sale, the buyer owes the seller that amount of money, as the tank and the oil in it come with the house. The settlement statement adds to the buyer's cost the price of the heating oil in the tank, and adds the same amount to the proceeds due to the seller.

Another cost in settlement on the HUD-1 is for property taxes. Typically, the annual taxes are prorated for each party, and, if the seller already paid all or part of the taxes, the HUD-1 shows the buyer's prorated share in the settlement section.

If you are paying off other debts with the proceeds of the mortgage, the HUD-1 will list each one, including your old mortgage. Among the closing documents, there should be a "payoff letter" for each debt listed. All payoff letters request written release of any liens, which the creditor must, by law, provide within sixty days.

The HUD-1 specifies the amount of money, if any, that you will either receive from the closing, or the amount of money you will need to bring to the closing in the form of a certified or cashier's check or cash. Your loan originator should have informed you of these amounts in advance. If you are refinancing and taking cash out, be aware that you will not walk away from the closing with cash in hand that you can spend immediately. Your refinance transaction is subject to the *right of rescission rule*, which states that you have three business days to cancel the deal without penalty. You won't get funds released to you until the rescission period is over. Then it may take several more business days for funds to clear after you deposit them with your bank before you can spend the money.

Prior to the closing, compare the GFE with the HUD-1 and question any differences in costs or fees that you see between the two. The numbers to which you agreed on the GFE should match closely the figures on the HUD-1. Ask your mortgage originator to review the

HUD-1 with you, in detail, before the closing. If you do not understand something, question it. And keep asking questions until you are satisfied with the explanations.

If you selected a good mortgage provider, you will be aware of and understand changes in terms or costs before you compare the GFE to the HUD-1. Remember, however, that the GFE is an estimate, and, on occasion, differences do occur. It is your right *and your responsibility*, as the captain of your financial ship, to raise the questions and get answers that satisfy you. If the terms are not what you expect and they are not acceptable, you have the right to refuse to close. Do not let the pressure of the closing dates and arrangements with closing attorneys intimidate you. Raise the issues you need to have addressed; if you don't, you may find yourself having to live with them for the next thirty years or until you sell your home or refinance. Keep your rate lock expiration date in mind, and consider the cost of losing your lock or paying additional extension fees if you delay the closing.

The Elements of the Mortgage Note

The *mortgage note* is the contract between you and the lender. All the terms and conditions of the loan are specified in the note, including the conditions under which the lender may foreclose. Read the note and check the rate of interest, the term of the loan, the adjustment periods and caps if you have an ARM, and the prepayment clause of the contract. There should be no surprises at this point.

If the mortgage note does not accurately reflect the terms you thought you were getting from the lender, do not sign. Any changes must be in writing and acknowledged in writing by all concerned parties. At the top of the note, you will see a loan number and the address of the property. This information should be included in any correspondence between you and the lender.

The mortgage note typically contains specific paragraphs that are explained in this section.

Borrower's Promise to Pay

The *Borrower's Promise to Pay* clause states that you promise to pay the principal amount as specified in return for a loan you received. It names the lender, and states that the lender may transfer the note, in which case you must make payments to the new note holder.

Interest

The *Interest* paragraph of the note specifies the annual percentage rate the lender will charge you on the unpaid principal balance. It also states that you agree to pay interest even if you default on the loan. If you have an ARM, this paragraph also states that the interest rate will change in accordance with details in the Interest Rate and Monthly Payment Changes section of the note.

Interest Rate and Monthly Payment Changes (ARMs Only)

The *Interest Rate and Monthly Payment Changes* section of the mortgage note for ARMs contains all the information related to the timing and rates at which your mortgage interest rate can be adjusted. It is organized into several paragraphs that each addresses a specific aspect of the allowed changes.

Change Dates. The *Change Dates* paragraph specifies the first date on which the interest rate can change, which marks the end of the period during which the initial interest rate is in effect. It also states how often after that the rate may change, usually once every twelve months from the end of the initial rate period.

Index. The *Index* paragraph specifies which of the several industry-accepted indices will be used to establish the starting point for the calculation of your interest rate on each change date. This paragraph is very specific about where the index is reported, and on what day, relative to the change date, the index value will be decided.

Calculation of Changes. The *Calculation of Changes* paragraph specifies the margin that will be added to the index to determine your new rate of interest until the next change date. It may also specify that it will round up the resulting rate to the next highest .125 percent. This paragraph also states that the lender will compute a new monthly payment amount sufficient to allow you to repay the loan in full by the maturity date.

Limits on Interest Rate Changes. The *Limits on Interest Rate Changes* paragraph documents the various caps to which your loan adjustments are subject. It states the highest and lowest interest rate at the end of the initial rate period (initial rate cap), the maximum amount by which the rate can change on any other change date (periodic cap), and the highest interest rate you could ever pay, which is based on the lifetime cap.

Effective Date of Changes. The *Effective Date of Changes* paragraph states that your new monthly amount takes effect on the change date, and that your next payment following the change date must be for the new amount.

Notice of Changes. The *Notice of Changes* paragraph states that the lender is obligated to notify you in writing, in advance of changes to your rate and monthly payment amount. It also states that the lender will provide you with contact information for one of its representatives who can answer your questions.

Payments

The *Payments* paragraph specifies the day of the month on which your monthly payment is due, the date on which your first payment is due, and the date when the final payment is due. It says that you will pay principal and interest and any other charges detailed in the note. The paragraph also specifies the amount of the monthly payment, and the address to which the payment should be sent.

Borrower's Right to Prepay

The *Borrower's Right to Prepay* clause is important to review, as it directly affects your ability to sell or refinance your home without penalty. This paragraph specifies any charges or penalties you must pay if you make payments on the principal before they are due. Prepayment penalties are common for mortgages to people who are poor credit risks. Some mortgages to people with good credit also have prepayment penalties, which are included to offset a slight decrease in interest rate. Most prepayment penalties are in effect only for the first three to five years of the mortgage. If there is no penalty for prepayment, it specifies that you can make principal payments at any time before they are due, as long as your scheduled monthly payments are up-to-date, and that you should notify the note holder in writing that you are doing so.

It also states, for a fixed-rate mortgage, that monthly payment amounts will not change if you make prepayments. When you pay extra toward the principal before it is due on a fixed-rate mortgage, the balance is zero before the maturity date. You will have fewer payments to make, and will have paid less in interest than if you make no prepayments. The biweekly payment option is a form of prepayment.

With an adjustable-rate mortgage for which you prepay principal, when your interest rate adjusts, the new monthly payment amount reflects the reduction in principal that resulted from your prepayments.

Loan Charges

The *Loan Charges* paragraph states that if the law changes and the interest rate on the note is greater than the new legal limit, the lender will reduce your interest on future and past payments. The lender has the choice to refund or apply as a prepayment any amounts owed you.

Borrower's Failure to Pay as Required

The *Borrower's Right to Pay as Required* paragraph, which states the rules for payment and the grounds for default, is important to read and understand. It specifies the latest day of the month by which the note holder must *receive* your payment to avoid late charges. It also states the percentage of the overdue payment that you will have to pay as a late charge. Do not leave your payments to the last day of this "grace period." Provide plenty of time if you are sending payments by mail. If you have to delay your payment close to the end of the grace period, check with your lender for options to make payments online or by phone to avoid late fees.

This clause clearly states that if you do not make your full monthly payment by the due date, you are in default. The due date is not the date on which your grace period ends, so technically the note holder can hold you in default if your payment is one day beyond the due date. While that is not likely to happen, don't even think of operating there.

In addition, this paragraph explains how the lender must notify you if you are in default. The notification will state that you have until a specified date (at least thirty days after the notice of default) to pay the overdue amount, and that if you fail to do that, the lender has the right to demand payment of the principal balance IN FULL, and to demand payment of any interest you owe. If the lender chooses not to exercise its right to demand payment in full, it does not lose the right to do so if you are in default again in the future.

If you are in default, in addition to demanding payment of the principal in full, you will be liable for legal costs, such as attorney's fees, incurred by the lender to enforce the note.

Giving of Notices

The *Giving of Notices* paragraph provides the address to which the lender will send all notices. It is normally the address of the property for which the note is held, unless you notify the lender (in writing) to send notices to a different address. The clause also offers information as to where to send notices to the lender.

Obligations of Persons Under This Note

If you have a co-borrower on the mortgage, the *Obligations of Persons Under This Note* clause specifies that each of you is liable for the full amount of the loan, and that the lender can go after each of you for full payment of the note if payment is overdue. Co-borrowers do not divide the mortgage liability; they share it in full.

Waivers

The *Waivers* paragraph relieves the lender of the obligation to notify others publicly that your payments are overdue. It also releases the lender from being required to demand payment in full if your payments are overdue.

Uniform Secured Note

The *Uniform Secured Note* clause references the Security or Mortgage Deed, which is the lien against your property. This paragraph specifies the conditions under which you may be required to pay the out-standing principal balance in full. One such condition is that if you sell the property, you must pay the balance at that time. Assuming you are able to sell your home for more than you owe, the proceeds of the sale will provide you the funds you need to do so.

Signatures

At the closing, you, any co-borrowers, and the lender sign the Mortgage Note. The signatures must be notarized and signed by an additional witness.

The Purpose and Importance of the Mortgage Deed

The *mortgage deed* is the document filed with the town clerk or other governing body to record the lender's lien against your property. It allows the lender to foreclose on your property if you default on the loan. This legal document spells out the security rights of the mortgage holder in legal language. It states that the property covered by the lien includes replacements, additions, improvements, and fixtures on the property, and it details items for which you must pay, such as hazard insurance, and, in some cases, property taxes. It also states items for which the lender will collect escrow funds from you and for which it will pay from those funds. The lender has the right to accumulate escrow balances in excess of the estimated costs for these items to protect its interests in case costs rise or your payment is late. RESPA dictates the maximum amounts the lender can put into escrow.

The *Property Insurance* section of the deed says that the lender determines what insurance coverage you must carry, and that you must pay for it. If you fail to carry the required insurance, the lender has the right to purchase it for you and charge you for it. All insurance policies that the lender requires must list the lender as the mortgagee or additional loss payee. This means that if you suffer a loss covered by insurance, the lender has an interest in the proceeds and can hold them pending repair of the damage. This clause specifically states that you must restore the property, and the lender has the right to determine whether the repairs are adequate.

The deed specifies that you are obligated to maintain your property to protect its value. The lender has the right to inspect your property, including the interior, if it has reason to believe you are not maintaining the property.

The deed warns that if you provided false statements on the loan application or during the loan application process, you are in default. This includes your statement regarding use of the property as your primary residence.

If you fail to perform your responsibilities, the lender can take action to protect its interest in your property, including making necessary repairs. The lender can add to your debt the cost for these repairs or for legal actions required to protect its interest, and this additional debt is subject to interest charges.

What Happens If You Are in Default

If you are in default, the lender has the right to "accelerate" the note, which means it can demand payment in full. The deed specifies the process of acceleration, which precedes foreclosure. The deed has an acceleration clause, a remedies clause, and a clause that states the borrower's right to reinstate after acceleration.

The *acceleration clause* spells out the written notice of default that the lender must provide you, the action you must take, and the date by which you must act to cure the default (a minimum of thirty days).

It states that your failure to take the prescribed actions within the defined period will result in acceleration and foreclosure or sale of the property. The notice of default also tells you how to reinstate good standing after acceleration, and the rights you have to contest the default. Note that the lender can add to your debt any fees it incurs while attempting to collect the default or exercise its right to foreclose or sell.

The deed describes your right to reinstate and force discontinuance of the foreclosure or other default action. It tells you the dates and/or events before which you may reinstate, and the conditions you must meet: pay all past due amounts, pay all expenses incurred from enforcing the agreement, and provide assurances to the lender that timely payments will continue to be made.

Other Documents in the Closing Package

The closing package contains many other documents, all of which you should read and understand before signing. Many of these documents are similar to or the same as those you signed when you submitted your mortgage application. You have the right to review in advance all the closing documents you will be required to sign. Many of them inform you of your rights. Some are acknowledgments you sign, indicating you received information. Question anything you don't understand, and don't sign until you do.

Truth in Lending Agreement

The Truth in Lending Agreement (TILA), which shows the APR, is one of the documents contained in both the application package and the closing package. If the costs for your loan changed between the GFE and the HUD-1, your APR may change as well. Check these numbers; compare them to the TILA in your application package, and understand the differences before signing. The closing TILA docu-

ment includes an itemized statement of the amounts financed as an
addendum to the APR information.

Monthly Payment Letter

At your closing, you will receive a *Monthly Payment Letter* that contains instructions regarding how to pay your mortgage: to whom it is
payable, where and when to make the payment, and the amounts of
principal, interest, tax escrow, PMI, and any other escrowed amounts
to which you have agreed. The instructions may direct you to make
payments to a party other than the lender with whom you close the
mortgage, because lenders often outsource the loan to third parties
for servicing. You may receive temporary payment coupons to use
when remitting your first few payments. These temporary coupons
give the servicing company time to set up your loan.

Loan Closing Disclosure Acknowledgment

By signing the *Loan Closing Disclosure Acknowledgment,* you acknowledge that the process by which you obtained the mortgage conformed
to RESPA requirements, which include the Good Faith Estimate and
Truth in Lending documents, and that you did not suffer discrimination. It also states that you have been notified of your rights should
the servicing of your loan transfer to another party, that you were
informed of the escrow requirements, insurance obligations and
rights, and that you acknowledge that the agreement is binding.

First Lien Letter

The *First Lien Letter* advises the lender that the loan has closed, and
that there is now a valid lien on the property because of the mortgage.

Hazard Insurance Authorization and Requirements

The *Hazard Insurance Authorization and Requirements* document details the lender's minimum insurance coverage requirements for your

property. It states that if you fail to provide and maintain that type and level of coverage, the lender has the right to secure insurance on your behalf, and you are obligated to pay for it.

Hold Harmless Mortgage Survey

The *Hold Harmless Mortgage Survey* releases the lender from responsibility for the status of insulation, well, and septic systems. It states that the lender has no obligation with regard to these items.

Tax Information Sheet

The *Tax Information Sheet* lists all the property-related taxes for which you are responsible. In addition to local real estate property taxes, you may be responsible for county property taxes, as well as special taxes for schools, sewers, or water.

Flood Insurance Notification

The *Flood Insurance Notification* document advises you that the lender will monitor data from FEMA concerning flood zone boundaries. Even if your property is not in a flood zone requiring insurance, this document notifies you that if FEMA changes the designation for your property in the future so it is within a zone requiring flood insurance, you are obligated to obtain and pay for it. If you fail to obtain flood insurance when required, the lender has the right to obtain it for you and make you pay for it.

Navigating the Mortgage Minefield: The Lender's "Say So" Doesn't Mean It Is So

A colleague who had been living in his home for ten years received notice that his property was now in a flood zone. The lender indicated that it would obtain $2,700 of flood insurance on his behalf if he failed to do so within a specified period. He called the insurance department of the mortgage company and asked what had prompted the notice. When he was unsatisfied with the lender's vague answer that "FEMA must have changed something," the lender told him to dispute the change with FEMA. The FEMA website showed no change to the flood zone map containing our colleague's property in eighteen years, and a FEMA representative confirmed it. Confronted with this information, the lender advised our colleague to obtain an exemption document from FEMA requiring a professional land survey, a ton of paperwork, and several months to obtain. Rejecting this option, our colleague escalated the issue to the lender's insurance supervisors and managers, until someone looked at the FEMA maps, acknowledged that the property was not and never had been in a flood zone, and filed the paperwork to remove the insurance requirement. It took several months and many more phone calls and follow up until computer-generated letters and statements no longer demanded insurance and the issue was finally resolved. The moral of this story? Don't assume the mortgage company is always right. Check everything, be persistent, and don't settle for explanations that don't make sense. You could save thousands of dollars.

Hazard Insurance Notification

If you are refinancing, the *Hazard Insurance Notification* letter informs your insurance company that your lender has changed. Your insurance policy names the lender in the policy's Mortgagee Clause, and this letter informs your insurance provider to update their records.

RESPA Servicing Disclosure

When you sign the *RESPA Servicing Disclosure*, which states that the lender may sell the servicing rights to your loan, you say that you are aware that the lender must notify you if that occurs. If you have a complaint about servicing, this document tells you how to resolve it.

Affidavit of Occupancy

The *Affidavit of Occupancy* is a document that states whether the property will be your primary residence, secondary residence, or an investment.

Borrower's Certification and Authorization

The *Borrower's Certification and Authorization* document asserts that you applied for the mortgage, that you know that false statements are illegal, and that you grant the lender permission to obtain records about information you provided on the application, such as assets, employment, and credit.

Privacy Notice

The *Privacy Notice* tells you with whom the lender will share your information (if anyone), and how you can prevent that sharing.

Congratulations! Now that you are familiar with all the paperwork needed for your closing, you can sign with confidence, fully responsible for the terms and conditions to which you are agreeing.

CHAPTER

STAY ABREAST OF CHANGES REGARDING YOUR MORTGAGE

The mortgage closing marks the beginning of your long-term relationship with the lender and the servicing company that will process your monthly payments. Over the course of any long-term relationship, circumstances change, events trigger the need for action, people make mistakes, and things can go wrong. The information in this chapter will alert you to these potential dangers so you can continue to safely navigate throughout the term of your mortgage.

In this chapter you will learn about:

☑ Commonly occurring changes after closing that can affect you

☑ Events that change your escrow payments and balances

Commonly Occurring Changes After Closing That Can Affect You

A few weeks after your closing on the home you purchased, you will receive the title and deed to your property. Put these papers in a safe place, such as a safe-deposit box.

Following your closing, two events commonly occur that can affect you: Your loan is sold to another lender, or your loan is transferred to a third party for servicing. In some cases, the lender services its own loans, but in others lenders sell the servicing rights to companies specializing in that field.

The mortgage note you signed at closing tells you to whom to make your monthly payments, and the party named is the loan servicer. A *loan servicer* is responsible for collecting and accounting for your mortgage payments, for maintaining records about escrow account payments made by you and on your behalf, and for providing you with annual documentation about the status of your loan. At closing, you also received notice of the RESPA requirements to which the lender and servicer must adhere if your loan is sold or if the servicer changes. If your lender sells your loan, the loan servicer probably will change, but even if the lender keeps your loan, it can change your servicer.

Both the current and new loan holder and servicer must provide you with advance written notification of a transfer, and must specify in detail any changes to your process for making payments to the new party or parties. By law, the terms of the mortgage note cannot change because of a sale of the note. The interest rates, balances, payment amounts, and due dates remain the same. The purchaser of your loan becomes the new lien holder on your deed, and becomes the mortgagee or additional loss payee on insurance policies required by the mortgage.

If your mortgage is sold, you receive notification in advance from both the original lender and the purchaser. The same holds true if your servicer changes; both parties involved in the transfer must notify you of the change. These notifications inform you as to when the change takes effect, the new address to which you submit your payments, and when to start sending payments there. Communications from lenders and servicers reference your original loan number, although a new lender and servicer are likely to assign you a new loan or reference number.

Once you receive notification of a change of lender or servicer, it is your responsibility to manage the delivery of your monthly payments to the correct party. Make sure the new amounts match the old, and check the grace period after which the new lender charges late fees. Update your written and computer records with the new address and payee for your mortgage payment.

If you are unsure about when or where you sent a payment during this transition period, or if you have a payment in transit, or if you make a mistake, notify by phone and in writing both parties, and call the proper party to verify that they received payment and credited it properly to your account.

If your lender automatically deducted your payment from your bank account, the new servicer may ask you to provide the routing information and account number, as well as an authorization to your bank allowing direct payments to the new servicer. Provide the necessary information and documents promptly; you do not want your payment to be late, because it will cost you late fees and damage your credit.

During this transition period, check your monthly mortgage statements carefully to make sure your accounts reflect all payments you have made. Follow up immediately if you see something unexpected or if payments are missing. If this is the case, follow up often and repeatedly until all records accurately reflect your payment activity. Document all phone calls, and follow up in writing if lenders or servicers do not act promptly.

When you get your first statement from the new lender or servicer, check all details carefully. Is the starting principal and interest rate accurate? Does the statement starting balance accurately reflect all payments that you have made to date? Are the escrow amounts and balances accurate? If so, you can settle back into your monthly routine. If not, pick up the phone immediately and be prepared to write and send a certified, return receipt letter explaining the discrepancies and enclose *copies* of all supporting documents. It may take some time to straighten out, and it is your responsibility to keep following up until the records are correct.

Navigating the Mortgage Minefield: Crazy Things Can Happen, but Don't Let Them Happen to You

No one likes junk mail, but pay attention to mail that claims to be about your mortgage, taxes, and other escrow items, even if it does not come from the party with whom you usually deal on these matters. Direct mail marketing has become quite sophisticated in designing envelopes that lead you to believe that the unsolicited offers inside are actually important information about your current mortgage. Regardless, open and look at it all. It could be information from the new lender or servicer that is important for you to act on; failure to do so could damage your credit and lead to foreclosure. In *The House of Sand and Fog*, a novel by Andre Dubois, a young woman who is irresponsible about tending to her mail loses her house and much more because of it. Does it mean you may have to open a lot of junk mail that you will throw away anyway? Yes. Do it. It is not worth risking your home to avoid this minor inconvenience.

The company that buys your loan or its servicing rights has people inspecting your account to identify changes needed to meet their standard operating policies and practices. They will notify you in writing, usually with a computer-generated letter, of the change they want to make. The letter will be authoritative, and you may think you have no say in the matter. You do. Whether it is insurance, tax escrows, PMI, or other aspects of your monthly payment, adjustment periods, and amounts, remember that neither a new lender nor a new servicer can change the terms of your loan as specified in the mortgage note. Ques-

tion everything you do not understand, and don't stop until you are
satisfied with the explanations.

Changes to Your Escrow Accounts

Most people with a mortgage pay a certain amount of their monthly
payment to fund escrow accounts used to pay real estate taxes, hazard
insurance, or PMI. Your loan servicer is obligated to provide you with
an annual statement of your escrow account balances. Several events
change your balance and the monthly amount you pay to escrow.

Real Estate Taxes

Your mortgage specifies that the servicer will collect the escrowed
funds for your real estate taxes from you. You pay your taxes to the
servicer in advance of when they are due to the tax collector. The
servicer puts your tax funds in an escrow account, and when the tax
bill is due, the taxes are paid from the funds in the escrow account.
You pay far enough in advance so that there are sufficient funds for
the servicer to pay the bill on time, even if your taxes increase or if
you are late with your payment. (Not YOU!)

You may never see the tax bill, which the servicer usually receives
directly from the tax collector. However, on the mortgage statement
following the tax payment you will see that the bill was paid and funds
were disbursed. Around the time the servicer pays the bill, it will
examine the actual amounts due, and anticipate the amount of the
next payment. If your escrow reserves are too low, or if the escrow
portion of your current monthly payment is not sufficient to cover the
anticipated bill, you will receive notification in writing that the
amount of your monthly escrow is increasing, and by how much.
This change in your monthly payment, resulting from an increase in

your taxes, can happen even if you have a fixed-rate mortgage. Remember that the fixed-rate applies only to the mortgage principal and
interest parts of your monthly payment, and other items, such as
taxes and insurance, can change.

Assessment and Revaluation. The real estate taxing body (city,
county, state) bases the amount of your tax bill on an assessment of
the value of your property. The assessed value may be the full market
value or some percentage of it. Your tax bill amount is computed by
multiplying the property assessment by what is called a "mill rate,"
which is a cost per thousand dollars of assessment. A mill rate of 13
mils means that you will pay $13 in taxes for every $1,000 of assessment. If your home has a fair market value of $200,000 and the
assessment represents 70 percent of the fair market value (as it is in
Connecticut), then a mill rate of 10 mils results in a tax bill of
$200,000 × .70 × .0010, or $1,400.

Because the taxing body cannot determine the fair market value of
every home every year, periodically it will conduct a property revaluation to adjust all property values in its jurisdiction. At this time it
adjusts all property assessments. The assessor will notify you or the
lender of the new assessment in advance, and will tell you the process
by which you can dispute the assessment. The period for appeals
usually lasts several months.

Pay attention. Keep abreast of market conditions in your area, particularly of the sale of homes similar to yours. When your assessment
notice arrives, read it, and understand how the assessment was determined. If you think the assessment is too high for the relative value
of your home, become familiar with the appeal process and use it.
The final assessment will stay in place until the next revaluation, so
whatever you do to reduce the assessment pays in the form of lower
taxes for years to come.

Improvements. You may need building permits to make improvements to your home, depending on the specific improvements and the laws that govern your home. The assessor may reassess your property upon completion of the improvements. If the assessment increases, so will your taxes, and the tax escrow amount you pay monthly with your mortgage.

Insurance

Any change in the value of your property can affect the amount of hazard, flood, and earthquake insurance coverage you must carry. If you make improvements to your home, review the amount of insurance you have purchased, and determine whether you need to increase it. Depending on the terms of your mortgage note, the choice may not be yours, but rather may fall within the lender's rights to determine. Refer to the mortgage note for your specific obligations. If you pay for your own hazard insurance, speak to your insurance professional to understand your coverage and determine your risk and additional insurance needs.

Under the terms of your mortgage, PMI cannot go up. However, your mortgage note specifies the conditions under which you may request removal of PMI. When your equity value reaches the minimum required to qualify for its removal, review all the requirements and request the removal when you have met them. You will have to know both the value of your home at the time the PMI was assessed and the amount of your current mortgage principal balance to know whether you are eligible for removal of the PMI requirement. For more details, refer to Chapter 10.

CHAPTER 13

WATCH MARKET TRENDS

Over the course of owning your home and paying your mortgage, real estate values will rise and fall, interest rates will rise and fall, and your income will change, either as you expect it to or unexpectedly. Your financial needs will change as your family situation changes; children grow and prepare for higher education, you get older and look toward retirement, your parents need care and financial support from you.

Since your home is likely to be the single largest asset in your financial portfolio, as your financial needs change, it makes sense to examine the opportunities that are available to you through the equity in your home. As real estate prices rise and your equity grows, you have the opportunity to take cash out for other investments or spending. As interest rates drop, you can lower your monthly cash outflow and redirect that money to other uses.

While no one can predict with certainty the future of real estate values or interest rates, there are signs to inform you about the short- and long-term choices you are likely to face.

In this chapter you will learn:

☑ What markets affect your equity and your choices for accessing it

☑ How inflation can affect your mortgage rate

☑ What other economic signs indicate changes in markets that affect the value of your home and your ability to tap into equity

☑ What the Housing and Economic Recovery Act of 2008 makes available to you and the impact it will have on your options for a mortgage in the future

What the Dow Jones Average Has to Do with Your Home

Financial markets, such as the stock markets, commodities markets, and bond markets, are closely related. As one performs better than another in the short term, investors pull money away from the poor performers and redirect it to the better performers. Likewise, as markets plunge or remain volatile, investors pull money out to invest in less risky markets.

Mortgages are an integral part of the bond market. Fannie Mae and Freddie Mac buy them in bulk and package them for sale as mortgage-backed securities on the bond market. If the stock market declines (as indicated by the Dow Jones Industrial Average and other measures), investors pull money out of stocks and put it into safer investments, such as U.S. Treasury notes, bonds, and mortgage-backed securities. The increased demand for these instruments raises the price of the bonds, and that lowers the effective interest rate, or yield, on the bonds. Mortgage interest rates follow.

As mortgaged-back securities become less attractive due to lower yields, money again funnels toward the stock market because its higher returns become more attractive. The decreased demand for bonds lowers their price. Investors demand higher rates of interest for the risk they are taking, increasing bond yield, and mortgage interest rates will rise.

Navigating the Mortgage Minefield: The Costly Cycle of Expanding and Contracting Borrowing Guidelines

Themortgagereport.com offers a very easy to understand explanation of the changes in lending policy that helped create the subprime mortgage crisis that spawned the Housing and Economic Recovery Act of 2008. Up until 2002, a limited number of people qualified for mortgages, and they were generally people with very good credit, assets, and income. In 2002 subprime lending began when lenders relaxed the mortgage qualification criteria, thereby expanding the number of people who could obtain mortgages and homes. As the loans performed well with few defaults, in 2003 lenders again relaxed the credit qualifying criteria, allowing even more people who previously were unqualified to buy homes. When these loans continued to perform well, yet a third round of relaxation of qualifying criteria took place in 2004, putting yet more people into homes.

Around 2005 subprime loans stopped performing well, and defaults became more common. In response, lenders tightened the mortgage qualification criteria to avoid the increasing risk of their former lending practices. That left people who could no longer qualify for a mortgage in homes, many with ARMs that were about to adjust. As defaults increased, additional rounds of qualification restrictions took place in 2006 and 2007, further limiting the number of home owners with refinancing options. The cycle continued, so that eventually, in 2008 only those borrowers with the highest credit and qualifications could qualify for loans, and a large number of home owners were ineligible for financing.

What does it mean to you? Everyone pays. If your credit, income, and assets are not great, it will be costly or impossible to obtain financing as qualifying criteria become more stringent. And even if your credit, income, and assets are excellent, lenders will eventually raise the cost of a mortgage to the most creditworthy borrowers to offset the risk and losses resulting from their past policies.

How Inflation Can Affect Your Mortgage Rate

The Consumer Price Index, which is calculated monthly by the Bureau of Labor Statistics (BLS), measures inflation. The BLS defines *inflation* as "changes in the prices paid by urban consumers for a representative basket of goods and services." Rapidly rising oil prices could mark the start of an inflationary period. Higher gasoline prices cause the transportation cost of food to rise, and as food costs and other living costs rise, there is pressure for wages to increase. Federal economy decision makers consider inflation a very serious economic risk. Money markets respond to inflation indicators by making the cost of money (interest rates) more expensive.

If you have an ARM, inflationary signals can indicate significant dangers ahead for you. Interest rates can increase rapidly, so review the terms of your mortgage, in particular the rate caps, and prepare accordingly. If you can refinance at a fixed rate, consider doing so.

As prices for basic commodities like food and gas rise, people on tight budgets who are just able to make mortgage payments face a cash flow problem, and may be unable to keep up with their mortgage payments. As the number of defaults increases, demand for mortgage-backed securities drops, causing the bond markets that issue them to raise interest rates to compensate investors for the increased risk. If mortgagees, already on the financial edge, then face increases in adjustable-rate mortgage interest rates, we have a vicious cycle of increasing rates and increasing defaults.

Inflation eats away at the future value of your investments. The money you have today that covers the cost of a year's worth of groceries, will not pay for as much when inflation occurs. If your assets don't increase in value at least as rapidly as inflation rises, you lose financial ground. As long as real estate prices rise as rapidly as inflation, your equity retains its purchasing power. If inflation rises and real estate values do not keep pace, the dollar amount of equity may rise, but it will do you less good. You are better off with $10,000 in equity when $10,000 can buy you enough food or gasoline for a year than you are with $20,000 in equity when, due to inflation, your $20,000 can't buy you twice as much.

Other Financial Indicators for You to Watch

The news regularly reports economic indicators that can help you stay abreast of opportunities to improve your financial position, or to avoid worsening it. Knowing how these factors, such as business activity levels, interest rates, regulatory legislation, and real estate values, affect you allows you to be proactive in determining your future.

Business Activity and Interest Rates

Interest rates are the indicator for the price of money, specifically credit. The higher the demand for credit, the higher interest rates go. What impacts the demand for credit? In a sluggish economy, people buy fewer things and demand for credit declines, bringing with it a decline in interest rates.

Housing starts, which measures the number of new homes being built, is another statistic regularly reported by the U.S. Census Bureau, and also influences interest rates. Increases in housing starts means greater demand for mortgages, and this generally predicts a strong economy and credit spending. As a result, interest rates tend to rise.

The Federal Reserve Board uses interest rates to regulate inflation and the supply of money (credit) for the country. If interest rates get too high, spending slows down and the economy gets sluggish. If interest rates get too low, people spend like crazy, and when too much money chases too few goods, inflation threatens. The *discount rate* is the rate of interest at which banks can borrow money from the Federal Reserve. The Federal Reserve raises and lowers the discount rate to counterbalance and regulate these trends. If the discount rate rises, the increase is passed on to consumers.

Prime Rate and Other Indices

If you have an adjustable-rate mortgage, your interest rate is a function of a specific index and the margin (an amount added to the index). Watch trends in the index to which your mortgage interest rate is tied, and be aware of when your adjustments take place. If necessary, consider converting to a fixed-rate mortgage.

Trends in Real Estate Values

The value of your home is affected by many factors locally, regionally, and nationally. While real estate values may be rising rapidly nationally, local factors, including the condition of your neighborhood and your home, have more influence over the price for which you could sell your home than broader economic factors.

It is important for you to monitor your equity position in your home. As long as you have positive equity, you can repay your mortgage by selling your home should you want or need to. Be aware of the value of your home as well. Given market conditions in your area and the specific strengths and drawbacks of your home, how much could you sell your house for, and is it enough to repay the balance of your mortgage? If it is not, you are "underwater" or "upside down" in your mortgage: You owe more than your home is worth. This situation greatly restricts your options. If you sell, you will have to cover the shortage with funds from other sources. If you stay, you will have to weather the storm and hope that values rebound (in the long term, historically they always do), because you will not be able to refinance.

When real estate values rise, you have the opportunity to tap into the equity in your home for major expenditures or other investments through refinancing, home equity loans, or lines of credit. Do not "max out" the debt you owe against the property. Property values can decline rapidly, and if you have borrowed to the limit, you may find yourself upside down and unable to reverse the situation.

The Housing and Economic Recovery Act of 2008 and What It Means to You

In July 2008, the U.S. Congress passed the Housing and Economic Recovery Act of 2008, to address the issues faced by the financial markets, government mortgage insurance programs, and individual home owners brought about by the circumstances that caused the subprime mortgage crisis.

The act contains three main areas of focus, each named a separate act, that deal with regulation of Fannie Mae and Freddie Mac, new FHA-insured loan programs, and a change to help prevent foreclosures.

Federal Housing Finance Regulatory Reform Act of 2008

This first component of the Housing and Economic Recovery Act of 2008 addresses issues related to Fannie Mae, Freddie Mac, and the *Federal Home Loan Banks (FHLB)*. The FHLB are twelve government-regulated regional banks that provide low-cost funding to other smaller banks for home, small business, and other loans. FHLB is a government-sponsored enterprise.

The first part of the act affecting these institutions establishes a new regulator for them to ensure good financial practices and standards. The regulator also has the authority to review and approve any new product offerings.

A second aspect of the act expands their ability to provide affordable housing to more people, in accordance with their mission. It raises the loan limits for conforming loans in high-cost areas (defined as areas where the median house prices are higher than the current limit of $417,000) to be in line with the current limit of $625,500 for Alaska, Hawaii, Guam, and U.S. Virgin Islands.

Other parts of the act include changes to the role these institutions play in home ownership and rental housing for low- and very-low-income families. It includes the creation of two funds, financed by contributions from Fannie Mae and Freddie Mac, to construct affordable rental housing.

FHA HOPE for Homeowners Act of 2008

The second act within the Housing and Economic Recovery Act of 2008 creates a new FHA program, HOPE for Homeowners (H4H). This temporary program allows banks to offer refinancing into FHA-insured loans at a significant discount to home owners at risk of foreclosure. One of the main goals of the program is to restore confidence in the credit markets by decreasing the uncertainty regarding the value of subprime loans, which will presumably put additional money into the credit markets.

Beginning October 1, 2008, and ending on September 30, 2011, the H4H program is available to any owner-occupants who cannot afford their mortgage payments, and who have a debt to income ratio above 31 percent. The thirty-year, fixed-rate loan amounts are based on what the borrower can afford, up to 90 percent of the value of the home, or a maximum of $554,440, and carry no prepayment penalties. Borrowers must demonstrate that they have sufficient steady income to meet the new H4H payments.

The H4H program is expected to help 400,000 home owners, and will insure $300 billion in mortgages but lenders have been very slow to participate in the program, which is voluntary for both borrowers and lenders. Any FHA-approved lender can offer loans under this program, but your current mortgage holder(s) must agree to accept the proceeds of the new loan as payment in full of your obligation. If you have been making payments under a loan workout or modification agreement, your application will receive extra consideration if and when lenders begin participating in the program.

The program releases neither lenders nor borrowers from the consequences of the loans that are not affordable. Lenders will sustain losses on the loans that are in trouble in order to benefit from the proceeds of these FHA-insured loans, but the losses are less than those they would suffer if they foreclosed. Borrowers do not get a free ride either. In exchange for relief, borrowers must split their newly created equity and appreciation in their home with the FHA, until the loan is paid or the home refinanced. And borrowers' access to their new equity is restricted, to be phased in over five years.

If you are in trouble, contact an FHA-approved counselor to help you begin the loan modification process with your mortgage holder as a prelude to the Hope for Homeowners option. Learn more about available programs and services at *www.MortgageModificationOnline .com.*

Foreclosure Prevention Act of 2008

The third component of the Housing and Economic Recovery Act of 2008 deals with government programs to prevent foreclosure and to assist communities affected by a large number of foreclosures. This component, called the Foreclosure Prevention Act of 2008, expands access to FHA-insured loans by increasing loan limits. It provides additional funds to communities hit hard by foreclosures to purchase foreclosed homes at a discount, and rehabilitate or rebuild them to stabilize the neighborhood and prevent additional loss of property values.

The Foreclosure Prevention Act also funds $150 million of housing counseling and $30 million in legal services to distressed borrowers. These funds are intended to facilitate borrowers and lenders or servicers to explore ways to keep the home owners in their homes.

The act also demands additional disclosures in connection with loan closings, including disclosure of all terms at least seven days in advance of closing to permit the borrower to shop for another loan, and new disclosures that specifically state the maximum monthly payments possible under the loan.

Finally, the Foreclosure Prevention Act extends the rights of people actively serving in the military. It increases from ninety days to nine months the time following discharge during which a lender cannot initiate foreclosure proceedings. It also prevents interest rate increases for one year following discharge. The act also mandates counseling programs for service members, and increased guaranteed amounts for VA loans.

The Emergency Economic Stabilization Act of 2008 and How It Affects You

In October 2008, after the failure of several financial institutions, the U.S. Congress moved to take control of the financial markets to restore confidence in them, and to restore the flow of credit that is essential to the national and global economy. The Emergency Economic Stabilization Act of 2008 (EESA) provides $700 billion for the U.S. Treasury to buy "troubled assets" from banks, Fannie Mae, Freddie Mac, and other financial institutions. Some of these "troubled assets" are subprime mortgages, or mortgages at risk for default and foreclosure.

The purpose of the act is that it "Provides authority to the Treasury Secretary to restore liquidity and stability to the U.S. financial system and to ensure the economic well-being of Americans." EESA has five major objectives:

☑ Stabilize the economy through the purchase of troubled assets and the availability of asset insurance;

☑ Preserve home ownership for American families wherever possible by requiring the modification of loan terms and expanding eligibility into the HOPE for Homeowners program;

☑ Protect taxpayers by requiring companies that sell troubled assets to the government to provide warrants or collateral;

☑ Establish penalties and preventive measures so that executives responsible for the troubled assets do not receive excessive compensation;

☑ Require frequent and detailed reporting to Congress by the Treasury, which will be monitored by an Oversight Board and a special inspector general to prevent arbitrary decisions and avoid waste, fraud, and abuse.

What does it mean to you? In the face of the collapse of the subprime mortgage market, many legislators are crying for credit reform, particularly in the mortgage industry. Most of the suggested regulatory changes raise standards of creditworthiness, reducing the risk and number of defaults. If you qualified for your mortgage when qualifying guidelines were less stringent, you may be unable to refinance, even if your financial position is as good as or better than it was at the time you obtained your mortgage. Consider the impact of these proposed changes in mortgage lending practices:

- ☑ Eliminate stated income loans and require income verification for all loans.

- ☑ Require lenders to assure that borrowers put money aside for taxes and insurance,

- ☑ Force lenders, when assessing a borrower's ability to pay, to assure that there are sources of funds besides the value of the home.

These regulations, if adopted, will remain in effect for many years. If you have an adjustable-rate or hybrid mortgage and are counting on being able to refinance when your introductory period ends or before the interest rate cap is reached, stay apprised of these discussions so you can act appropriately.

Under this act the government is putting pressure on lenders to avoid foreclosures, and is offering programs that are designed to help homeowners get caught up on delinquencies and stay current with their mortgage payments. In addition to FHA-insured loans described in Chapter 14, the government can provide special forbearance arrangements for up to 36 months during which mortgage payments may be suspended while you restore your financial stability. If you owe more than your home is worth, you may be eligible for a *short refinance*, which is a reduction in principal owed to reduce your monthly payments. Qualified veterans can obtain a special modification in which the delinquent amount is added to the principal and the loan is re-amortized, resulting in a lower monthly payment.

CHAPTER 14

WHAT CAN GO WRONG,
AND HOW TO FIX IT

Even if you exercised due diligence when obtaining your mortgage by budgeting responsibly and saving for extra costs, circumstances can prevent or make it difficult for you to meet your financial obligations. Illness, job loss, divorce, or the death of a loved one or the income earner in the family could cause you to miss a payment, be late with a payment, or be unable to pay your mortgage for several months or more.

In this chapter you will learn:

☑ Relief available in case of natural disaster or active military duty

☑ Actions to take and options available if you face financial hardship

☑ Last resort options to avoid foreclosure

Relief During Temporary Disruptions

Certain events beyond our control can have an immediate and devastating impact on our ability to meet our financial obligations. Lenders will, either through negotiation, or as a result of legal requirements, grant borrowers some relief if they are victims of a natural disaster, or are called to active military duty.

Natural Disaster Relief

If you suffer a natural disaster such as a flood, hurricane, or earthquake, and your property is within a declared disaster area, in most cases your lender will work with you by suspending late fees, not reporting late payments to credit agencies, and delaying foreclosure action against you. If you have an FHA-approved loan, the lender is obligated to grant you these measures.

Active Military Duty

If you or your spouse are serving in the military, you may be able to temporarily reduce your interest rate, and hence your monthly payment, while you are on active duty. The Servicemembers Civil Relief Act (SCRA) specifies the maximum interest rate a lender can charge a member of the military on active duty (currently 6 percent). You must ask for the rate reduction in writing; your lender will not grant it to you automatically. The time period during which you can make this request is limited, so don't delay. You can make the request as soon as you get your active duty orders, which you will have to show to the lender. The lender forgives the reduced interest under the terms of SCRA, so you do not have to make up the interest payments in the future. However, your interest rate returns to the original terms of your mortgage ninety days after your active duty ends.

A lender is not allowed to initiate foreclosure procedures while you are on active duty, or for those ninety days following completion of active duty, unless it can prove that your active duty did not impact your ability to pay your mortgage. If you cannot meet your payments even at the reduced interest rate under SCRA, the lender can find ways to keep you in your home. For example, it can allow you to make interest-only payments while on active duty and pay the principal in the future to get you through the rough spot. If you need assistance, seek out Armed Forces Legal Assistance at http:// legalassistance.law.af.mil/ content/locator.php to find an advisor in your area.

What to Do If You Are Facing Financial Hardship

One of the biggest mistakes people make when they realize they are in financial trouble is to do nothing. Seek help sooner rather than later, as the farther behind you get, the harder it is to catch up, and the greater the likelihood that you will damage your credit.

Acknowledge you have a problem. Don't ignore the problem or hope it will go away. Don't be unduly optimistic to justify delaying the unpleasant task of facing your financial problems. "I think things will improve so I'll just wait a couple of weeks," goes the dangerous thinking. Don't delay. The longer you wait, the fewer your options.

Go Back to the Basics of Budgeting

If you face financial hardship, go back to the basics of budgeting. Prioritize your expenses—including food, shelter, and utilities—and cut back on non-essentials; it could provide you with enough extra money to meet your obligations. Consider selling assets to raise cash for your mortgage; you can turn stocks, other investments, second cars, and boats into money to pay your mortgage and keep your home. Although you may have to forego paying other bills, keep in mind that this will damage your credit. Negotiate with creditors to reduce your monthly payments. Remember that free or low-cost credit counseling is available.

If you are embarrassed, think about how much more embarrassed you will be if you lose your home. If you are afraid that by admitting a problem your lender will start proceedings against you, remember that the lender does not want to foreclose on your property unless your equity is a substantial percentage of the value of the property. Foreclosure is a costly, time-consuming process that is bad for customer relations. Your lender prefers that you make payments, to keep you in your home, and to preserve as much profit on your loan as possible.

Review the terms of your mortgage note to know what constitutes default and what rights the lender has if you fall behind. Remember that your lending institution has a legal, binding contract and is not required to do anything to accommodate your problem. Regardless of the circumstances that caused your financial problems, you are still responsible for meeting your obligations, and there are no excuses that justify non-payment.

Loss Mitigation Options

Loss mitigation services are rapidly becoming a normal part of the mortgage industry, and involve over a trillion dollars in loans. *Loss mitigation* involves the negotiation of temporary or permanent changes in payment terms to avoid foreclosure. If you find yourself needing this service, you are wise to keep in mind that your mortgage lender is in business to make a profit, and will do everything possible to protect its bottom line first. Your mortgage lender will offer you a mortgage modification plan that preserves its profit.

Loss mitigation as an industry is less regulated than mortgage lending, which should raise concerns. Unfortunately, more and more people need loss mitigation services, and lenders are more and more difficult to deal with, as volume increases and losses mount. And negotiating with your lender when you are behind in your payments is like being represented by the attorney you hit in an auto accident. In spite of all protestations to the contrary, the bank is going to represent its own interests, not yours, when negotiating with you. If you are dealing with representatives from the bank's customer service department, understand that their job is to collect or get commitments for payments, regardless of your circumstances. If you reach the bank's loss mitigation department, know that its job is not to keep you in your home, but to negotiate a workout agreement that best protects the bank's investment, which may be one that keeps you in your home.

Government housing agencies can negotiate with lenders on your behalf, but they are woefully understaffed causing long delays, and staff have little training in loss mitigation or negotiation. They also have no personal stake in getting you a modification that works for you, as staff get paid whether they negotiate successfully on your behalf or not. However, the FDIC recently suggested that lenders pay housing agencies for successful negotiations, which raises the serious question of where the agency's fiduciary responsibility lies.

Get help from an outside source. There are many ways for you to work out your payments but you must know how and who you should get to work for you. Your bank is not on your side. Your bank is looking out for its own interests, as it should. You need a professional looking out for you; someone who has a stake in achieving an agreement.

You don't have to pay for advice concerning how to avoid foreclosure, but you only get what you pay for. A good, reputable firm gets paid if it succeeds at negotiating a solution for you and may ask for a small upfront application fee of three to five hundred dollars to show your good faith to provide the necessary information at the time it is needed so negotiations can move forward.

There are reputable mortgage companies who can analyze your situation, explain your options, help you prepare the documentation you will need, and handle the negotiations with the lender on your behalf. Experienced loss mitigation negotiators know how to work with lenders and complex loss mitigation departments to get you into a position to keep your home and honor your financial commitments. Reputable firms will not charge you a fee (other than an application fee) unless they achieve a successful modification on your behalf. As an unbiased third party expert without emotional attachment, they can present your hardship effectively to the right people, and are better able to negotiate hard and bring to closing a permanent modification.

Some people consider hiring an attorney to renegotiate the terms of their mortgage, assuming that attorneys are skilled at negotiation. But unless an attorney is experienced in the specific area of loss mitigation, with lots of experience negotiating with specific lenders for mortgage modifications, it is almost impossible to know whether the terms the lender is proposing are the best terms and comparable to those offered to other borrowers in similar circumstances.

A loss mitigation specialist knows what options are available in this new market, and will press for the solution that best meets your needs. He or she will escalate your case to a higher level in the lender's organization than the people who deal directly with borrowers who are unlikely to have the authority to negotiate or approve the type of plan you need to meet your obligations.

Professionals know what to say, when to say it, and understand your lender's motivation, all of which increases your chances for success at getting an affordable loan modification agreement. The process of negotiating a loan modification with your lending institution is no easy task. Many homeowners who tried it on their own before going to a professional have reported that identifying and getting through to the correct person in the right department was nearly impossible. They spent hours on the phone for each call, and there were many.

Seventy percent of homeowners pursuing a loan modification directly with their bank will wind up with a *repayment* or *forbearance* plan, which are most profitable for the lender. These plans generally require both a lump sum payment and higher monthly payments for several months until your account is up to date. The bank may also tack on fees and other charges to the balance you owe and must repay.

Think about it. Unless your inability to pay your mortgage was a one-time, short-lived interruption in your otherwise healthy financial life, depleting your savings and increasing your monthly payments is not likely to solve your problem, and you are likely to end up in trouble again. The bank's immediate problem, on the other hand, is nicely solved with these loss mitigation offerings.

If your financial problems are longer-term or permanent, you still have options, but you need the assistance of a professional to close the deal with your lender. A temporary *loan modification* can get you relief for a year or two during which the lender will temporarily accept a lower interest rate to reduce your monthly payment. At the end of the agreement, your mortgage will revert to its original terms.

When you have a professional loss mitigator working for you, your lender may be willing to permanently change your mortgage terms to lower your monthly payments by changing the interest rate, converting an ARM to a fixed-rate mortgage, or by extending the term. Rarely, a lender will also agree to reduce the principal you owe. Permanent modifications are permanent losses for the lender, so they are not readily offered. If you made principal prepayments on a fixed-rate mortgage, you did not reduce your monthly payment, but you are on target to pay off your mortgage sooner than its maturity date. If this is the case, your lender can recast your remaining balance to the original maturity date, thereby reducing your monthly payment.

Navigating the Mortgage Minefield: Beware: Loss Mitigation is the Latest in Unregulated Marketing Practices in the Mortgage Industry

Most people in need of loss mitigation are hard-working people who are facing difficult financial circumstances. Very few people seeking loss mitigation advice are looking for a government handout or to take advantage of the current financial crisis. The purpose of the government bailouts is not to release borrowers or lenders from their obligations; it is not a handout, but an obligation for both borrowers and lenders to work out agreements that minimize foreclosures.

If you believe that poor regulatory oversight is responsible for the current mortgage industry mess, the marketing abuses that are breeding in the loss mitigation market will terrify you. Head's up! Here are some true stories from clients regarding questionable tactics and ploys banks and lenders are using to meet their obligations to offer workouts, while attempting to get distressed borrowers to agree to a workout or modification that is most profitable to the lender:

- ☑ A bank recently sent a letter to delinquent borrowers telling them to sign and return the enclosed modification/forbearance agreement with a payment to receive a $200 American Express gift card

- ☑ Banks won't put agreements into writing until after payments are made, or won't put the agreements in writing at all

- ☑ Banks demand post-dated checks

- ☑ Harassing phone calls demanding payment and threatening foreclosure

- ☑ Pressuring borrowers into feeling guilty so they agree to lesser terms

Again, more than ever, you need to work with companies who are reputable and experienced. And you should seek professional loss mitigation assistance from a party other than your bank or lender. Reputable firms stand the test of time, and the referrals and recommendations they receive from clients and other industry professionals come from a consistent record of service, expertise, and integrity. Check with the Better Business Bureau to know whether you are dealing with a reputable firm. For more information and a free loan modification analysis, visit www.Mortgage ModificationOnline.com.

FHA-Insured Loan Options. If you meet certain requirements and you have an FHA-insured loan, you may qualify for a one-time, interest-free loan through HUD to bring your mortgage current. To be eligible you must be at least four—yes at least four—but not more than twelve months delinquent in your monthly payment, you must have overcome the circumstances that led to your default, and you must occupy the home as your primary residence. The loan is called a partial claim, and is in the form of a promissory note, and is another lien against your property. Payment is due to HUD when you sell your home or pay off your first mortgage.

If All Else Fails

If there is no way you can keep your home, you may still be able to avoid foreclosure and the damage it does to your credit. For instance, a professional negotiating on your behalf may get your lender to agree to a *pre-foreclosure sale*, which gives you time to sell your home and pay off the amount you owe on your mortgage. Or, if the market value of the property won't cover the amount you owe, the lender may be convinced to accept a *short-sale*, which means the lender accepts the proceeds from the sale and forgives the remaining balance. Finally, the lender may agree to a *deed-in-lieu of foreclosure*, which means the lender takes the deed to your home instead of foreclosing, and forgives the debt. While you do not keep your home, these options are less damaging to your credit than foreclosure.

CONCLUDING COMMENTS

You now have the information and knowledge that will guide you safely through the mortgage minefield. Whether your purpose is to obtain your first mortgage, have a better experience when you refinance, or find a way to keep your home and meet your obligations as you work out financial difficulties, you now can look at yourself and your options using the tools we've provided, so you can make informed and responsible financing decisions for yourself and your family.

When faced with an important decision in an area we think is outside our expertise, it is easier to let the experts tell us the right thing to do than it is to understand and be responsible for our choices. If things work out well we congratulate ourselves on our wise choice of experts. If things don't work out, we were misguided, ill-served and taken advantage of. Whether it is mortgage brokers, doctors, car salesmen, or bureaucrats, whenever we abdicate our decisions to others, rather than engage with them as partners to arrive at decisions for which we are fully responsible, we shortchange ourselves.

No book can prepare you for all the possible circumstances you could face as you negotiate your way into a home you can keep and a mortgage you can afford, or work to save the house you have. Market conditions and the political climate are volatile, and the rules of the game change frequently. There is no way to predict what will happen between now and the next time you seek mortgage financing.

Rather than provide you with a step-by-step instructional "how to" that would likely require updating between the completion of the manuscript and the time the finished book arrives on bookshelves, we've provided you with a compass—a tool with which you can guide your thinking, your actions, and your decisions, regardless of the specific rules and regulations in effect at any point in time. Because the rules and guidelines change often, each time you venture into the mortgage markets, rather than assume your knowledge is still valid, verify it by asking questions and getting the answers you understand.

You have the information, the tools, and the power to make home ownership a rewarding reality for you and your family. Regardless of upturns, downturns, shifts, slumps, or bubbles, you can navigate your way through to a decision that serves you and your family, so you can take pleasure in your home and the lifestyle it affords you.

Take charge and enjoy!

Appendix

Table A-1. Loan Comparison Worksheet

		Current Situation	What I want/ need	Loan Option A	Loan Option B
My Requirements					
1	**My Monthly Income**				
	Housing Expense				
2	Monthly mortgage/ Rent payment				
3	Taxes				
4	Hazard insurance				
5	PMI				
6	PMI expiration at $				
7	**Total Housing Expense (Total Lines 2 through 5)**				
8	**Housing Ratio (Line 7 / Line 1)**				
	Debt Accounts	Balance	Monthly Minimum		
9	Debt 1				
10	Debt 2				
11	Debt 3				
12	Debt 4				
13	Debt 5				
14	Debt 6				
15	Debt 7				
16	Debt 8				
17	**Total Debt (Total Line 9 through Line 16)**				
18	**Total Housing and Debt Expense**				
19	**Debt to Income Ratio (Line 18 / Line 1)**				
20	**Value of the home**				
21	Down payment or equity				
22	Balance owed on current mortgage				

Table A-1. Loan Comparison Worksheet (Continued)

		Current Situation	What I want/ need	Loan Option A	Loan Option B
23	Debt reduction amount				
24	Prepayment penalty				
25	Other cash out				
26	**Principal Amount**				
27	**Loan to Value Ratio (Line 26 / Line 20)**				
28	Minimum time in my home				
29	Minimum fixed payment period				
Offers					
30	**Lender Name**				
31	Contact				
32	Contact phone				
33	Contact email				
34	Contact FAX				
35	**Fixed or Adjustable?**				
36	**Term (years)**				
37	**Full Amortization Date**				
38	**Interest Rate (initial)**				
39	Prepayment penalty amount				
40	Prepayment penalty expiration date				
41	Total interest paid				
42	Points				
43	Fees				
44	Origination or Underwriting fee				
45	Lender or Funding fee				
46	Credit report				
47	Appraisal				
48	Rate lock expiration date				

Table A-1. Loan Comparison Worksheet (Continued)

		Current Situation	What I want/ need	Loan Option A	Loan Option B
49	Other fees related to credit				
50	"Amount Financed" for APR				
51	APR				
52	Time to closing				
	Costs at Closing/ Settlement				
53	Title (lender's)				
54	Title (mine)				
55	Attorney				
56	Document prep fees				
	Payment Options				
57	Extra principal?				
58	Biweekly?				
59	Balloon?				
60	Interest-only option?				
61	Minimum payment option?				
	Adjustable Rates				
62	First adjustment (months)				
63	Max first adjustment increase %				
64	Maximum payment after one year				
65	Frequency of adjustments				
66	Maximum increase in one adjustment				
67	Maximum increase over term				
68	Index				
69	Margin				

Index